UNLOCKING HEAVEN

BOOKS BY KEVIN DEDMON

The Ultimate Treasure Hunt

Unlocking Heaven

AVAILABLE FROM DESTINY IMAGE PUBLISHERS

UNLOCKING HEAVEN

KEYS TO LIVING NATURALLY SUPERNATURAL

Kevin Dedmon

© Copyright 2009 – Kevin Dedmon

All rights reserved. This book is protected by the copyright laws of the United States of America. This book may not be copied or reprinted for commercial gain or profit. The use of short quotations or occasional page copying for personal or group study is permitted and encouraged. Permission will be granted upon request. Unless otherwise identified, Scripture quotations are from the HOLY BIBLE, NEW INTERNATIONAL VERSION®. Copyright © 1973, 1978, 1984 International Bible Society. Used by permission of Zondervan. All rights reserved. Scripture quotations marked NASB are taken from the NEW AMERICAN STANDARD BIBLE®, Copyright © 1960, 1962, 1963, 1968, 1971, 1972, 1973, 1975, 1977, 1995 by The Lockman Foundation. Used by permission. Scripture quotations marked NKJV are taken from the New King James Version. Copyright © 1982 by Thomas Nelson, Inc. Used by permission. All rights reserved. Scripture quotations marked KJV are taken from the King James Version of the Bible. Emphasis within Scripture quotations is author's own. Please note that Destiny Image's publishing style capitalizes certain pronouns in Scripture that refer to the Father, Son, and Holy Spirit, and may differ from some publishers' styles. Take note that the name satan and related names are not capitalized. We choose not to acknowledge him, even to the point of violating grammatical rules.

DESTINY IMAGE® PUBLISHERS, INC.

P.O. Box 310, Shippensburg, PA 17257-0310

"Speaking to the Purposes of God for this Generation and for the Generations to Come."

This book and all other Destiny Image, Revival Press, Mercy Place, Fresh Bread, Destiny Image Fiction, and Treasure House books are available at Christian bookstores and distributors worldwide.

For a U.S. bookstore nearest you, call **1-800-722-6774.**

For more information on foreign distributors, call **717-532-3040.**

Or reach us on the Internet: **www.destinyimage.com**

ISBN 10: 0-7684-2750-9

ISBN 13: 978-0-7684-2750-9

For Worldwide Distribution, Printed in the U.S.A.

5 6 7 8 9 10 11 / 13 12 11 10

ACKNOWLEDGMENTS

I want to thank my wife, Theresa, who I love with all of my heart! You have inspired me to take more risks. You are the greatest revivalist I know.

Thanks to my amazing children, Chad, Julia, and Alexa, for going after your destiny. The way you pursue a revival lifestyle pushes me to go for more.

Thanks to Bill and Beni Johnson, Kris and Kathy Vallotton, and the rest of the Bethel team for encouraging me and releasing me to fulfill my dreams. You are all amazing revivalists and have pioneered a way for me to travel easier on the road of revival.

Thanks to my grammar doctor, Pam Spinozi, for your patience and prescriptions in curing my periodic, pitiable punctuation.

I want to thank Marla Baum and her team for partnering with me in intercession. I never leave home without them!

Finally, I want to thank all of the revivalists of history who have unlocked Heaven, leaving keys as an inheritance, so that their ceiling could be our floor.

ENDORSEMENTS

Kevin Dedmon has done it once again. His latest book, *Unlocking Heaven: Keys to Living Supernaturally,* provides powerful impartations and practical, real-life examples of how to live as a revivalist in any environment. This is a refreshing book that will empower you to live a life of miracles in a natural lifestyle. It is a must-read for any person serious about increasing personal faith by apprehending the realities of Heaven so they become normal life on planet Earth.

—Dr. Che Ho Ahn
Apostolic Leader and Senior Pastor of Harvest Rock Church
President of Harvest International Ministry

Kevin Dedmon's book, *Unlocking Heaven,* is the perfect blend between rich revelation, practical examples, and powerful testimonies. As a father in the Bethel movement, his life will spur spiritual sons and daughters to be ordinarily extraordinary and supernaturally natural. Miracles unto harvest is how we step into the darkness to see Jesus break forth in His glorious light. This book will empower and equip you to step into the "more" for which Jesus died.

—Heidi Baker
Director, Founding Director of Iris Ministries, PhD

I have always been a firm believer that God uses ordinary people to do extraordinary things. This book has come in due season because God is activating everyone in His presence who is willing to love and bring His nature on the earth. Kevin captures key moments in his own personal life that help the reader make the same key connections to simple truths that can unlock a world of perspective on how to pursue your own supernatural journey.

—Shawn Bolz
Expression58
Author of *Keys to Heaven's Economy* and
The ThroneRoom Company

In his first book *The Ultimate Treasure Hunt*, Kevin taught us how to supernaturally find treasure in the hearts of people who may have lost their way in the vortex of world circumstances. Kevin Dedmon's new book, *Unlocking Heaven,* reads like a five-star sequel to a great movie. His insights into awaking the power of God in the life of every Believer are astounding, revelatory, and yet remarkably simple. As you make your way through the pages of this book you will find yourself on a Holy Spirit journey in which you will be inspired to walk in miracles, empowered to do the works of Jesus and equipped with the boldness to go where you have never gone before! This book is a "must-read" for every serious Christian!

—Kris Vallotton
Co-founder of the Bethel School of Supernatural Ministry
Author of *Developing a Supernatural Lifestyle* and
The Supernatural Ways of Royalty

TABLE OF CONTENTS

FOREWORD

EVERY Wednesday morning our staff gathers for about three hours. It's my favorite meeting of the week. I love to spend time with this amazing team. Together we share the miracles we have seen in the last week or so. We also talk about what we're learning from the Holy Spirit about the realm of His miracle-working power. We usually cut off the reports after about two hours. To say it is encouraging is a great understatement. I constantly find myself turning to whoever is sitting next to me and saying, "Can you believe we get to be alive at a time like this?" We are experiencing more than I ever dreamed of as a young man.

Sometimes we learn by "drafting" on another person's experience. The team concept expands each person's opportunity to learn and be changed—especially when the culture of honor for one another is the glue that holds us together. One of the great truths regarding miracles is that ministering with people who have a great anointing for healing and deliverance affects what we are able to do. Their grace for miracles eventually becomes our own. Kevin Dedmon embraced this process with joy.

The Dedmon family moved to Redding several years ago after a brief visit. They resigned their pastoral position and became students in our Bethel School of Supernatural Ministry. Kevin was already a successful pastor with a great education, a heart for ministry, and a powerful anointing for evangelism. I don't know very many ministers who would be willing to do this, especially when you consider that this successful pastor and wife might be sitting next to someone in our school who was only a few months old in the Lord. But desperation for God causes people to do the unthinkable. It seems to be the way to break into the signs that make you wonder.

Their whole family thrived in this culture. Today Kevin and his wife, Theresa, are on our pastoral staff. The miracle anointing became their own as they sought God and humbled themselves to learn from those who were already functioning in that gift. Today Kevin has one of the strongest miracle anointings that I know of. And the really fun part of the story is that he is now training others to do the same, because it is never about us. Miracles are *not* to be the source of our self-esteem or identity. All of these manifestations of the Gospel are simply to bring glory to the Lord Jesus Christ. This book is a part of his passion to equip and release believers into their destiny of being used by the Holy Spirit.

This wonderful book was lived before it was written. The stories and truths were shared in our staff meetings and demonstrated in the context of Bethel Church family's pursuit of *more*.

The stories are stirring and provoking. It's hard to remain the same after hearing what God is doing in this day. Kevin's insights are strong and helpful. Having the mysteries of Scriptures opened up, as Kevin does for us, adds another element that fuels the passion for the display of the authentic Gospel. You will be changed by feeding yourself on this account of what happens when people choose to live a naturally supernatural life. *Unlocking Heaven* was written just for you.

—Bill Johnson
Senior Pastor of Bethel Church, Redding, CA
Author, *When Heaven Invades Earth* and
The Supernatural Power of a Transformed Mind

INTRODUCTION

I always thought of people in public ministry as having a special, supernatural anointing and ability that normal, everyday Christians could not access. When I entered public ministry in 1981, however, that myth soon vanished; I realized that I had no greater supernatural ability, even though I was a pastor. Neither did the other pastors I knew. In fact, many I knew in public ministry did not rely on supernatural empowerment at all, but on their own inherent charisma and natural talent.

I began to notice that many of the "great" revivalists throughout history began as very normal Christians with very normal backgrounds much like mine. For example, Smith Wigglesworth was a plumber before becoming one of the generals of the healing revival of the 1900s. John G. Lake was an executive in the insurance industry before becoming one of the greatest healing revivalists of the 1950s. William Branham worked for an electric company as a field maintenance and repair man and never even graduated from high school, yet he saw some of the most amazing miracles in the history of the Church.

Maria Woodworth-Etter was a stay-at-home mother before she helped usher in the Pentecostal Movement as an itinerant preacher who healed the sick wherever she went. Aimee Semple McPherson was the widow of a missionary and only reluctantly accepted an invitation to preach on a ship when no one else could be found.

I further noticed that Jesus did not ask for degrees and pedigrees when He began to consider accepting the disciples into training to become apostles (see Luke 6:12-16). In fact, we are told in First Corinthians 1:26-29 that He specifically called those who were common by worldly standards; they were normal people, representing every walk of life.

Soon I realized that I had the same invitation to change the world as the disciples of the Bible and the generals of revival throughout Church history. After all, what did they have that I do not have? I have the same Spirit they had. I have the same authority. The only difference is that they discovered the keys to unlock Heaven, which allowed them to live a naturally supernatural lifestyle.

Often in the past, even as a pastor, I felt like my prayers were hitting the ceiling. Even when they did get through, it seemed as though God had turned a deaf ear to my prayers for divine intervention. The heavens appeared to be closed when it came to seeing the supernatural, miracle-working power of God released. In the last several years, however, I have learned how to live in greater measures of Kingdom breakthrough.

This book is designed to offer some of the keys that I have found in my pursuit of unlocking Heaven and living a naturally supernatural life. I do not intend to imply in any way that these are all of the keys, but they are the ones that have unlocked Heaven for me. I am still pursuing more keys, and when I find more, I'll write another book!

I hope this book will be a resource for your pursuit in unlocking Heaven and living a naturally supernatural life, and I hope that every page will release an impartation that will propel you to the next levels as a world changer and revivalist. I pray that the keys that I have found will lead you to places in His presence that will reveal more keys that unlock Heaven. When you get them, please write a book so that I can buy it and be as blessed as I hope you will be as you read mine!

Chapter 1

LIVING A NATURALLY SUPERNATURAL LIFE

As I sat down in my aisle seat on the plane, I noticed a woman in the seat across from me holding a strange-looking sandwich-type thing. Sitting down, I asked, "What is that?" Holding up the unusual concoction, she responded, "It's a cabbage and tofu sandwich, do you want a bite?" to which I responded, "No thanks! I prefer a double cheeseburger." She then began to explain that, if I ate like her, I would live longer and healthier. I replied, "If I had to eat like that, I wouldn't *want* to live longer."

Over the next 20 minutes, she continued to try to convince me of the benefits of eating a vegetarian diet. I remained steadfast, however, and countered each point with a playful, joking argument of my own about the benefits of eating a greasy pepperoni pizza or barbeque beef sandwich. Meanwhile, her husband, sitting next to the window, pretended he was asleep.

After poking fun at each other's diets, we exchanged names, and she asked me what I did for a living. I responded, "I'm a healer."

Excitedly, she proclaimed that she was a healer of sorts as well.

When I asked her how she healed people, and what she healed people of, she said that she was a massage therapist, a yoga instructor, and a follower of the Dalai Lama.

She continued, "I help people get in touch with and become one with the universe around them and the universe within them. I teach them relaxing meditations and massage their bodies in order to reduce tension and stress. As they experience a greater level of peace in their mind and body, they begin to have less anxiety, causing a decrease in anxiety-related symptoms like hypertension and muscle tension."

With a confident smile, she asked, "How do you heal people, and what do you heal people of?"

I explained, "I channel. I invite God's presence into me, and then I leak Him out to people around me. When His presence touches people with things like cancer, asthma, fibromyalgia, broken bones, bulging discs, blindness, deafness, and deformities, they often get healed."

I then shared a testimony of how I had prayed for a girl who was missing her jawbone (she had had it surgically removed after a car accident completely shattered it). In prayer, I released God's presence, and she grew a new jawbone. I shared testimonies of how I had seen people healed of fourth-stage cancer after I had prayed for them. Her eyes continued to widen as I shared testimony after testimony of God's healing presence.

Finally, she looked at me and asked, "Do you think you could heal my husband?"

Without hesitation, I exclaimed, "Oh sure, no problem!"

How could I hesitate after I had just told her that I was a healer! I did, however, feel a sense of terror as it dawned on me that I had failed to ask what was wrong with her husband. He was still asleep, or pretending to sleep, and as I looked at him, he seemed to be healthy.

She then explained that he had a cancerous tumor in his left arm and that it was all the way to the bone. I didn't realize it at the time, but the cancer had also metastasized to the lungs, producing several nodules that appeared as though they would protrude through the skin. She went on to say that they had tried all sorts of naturopathic therapies, but nothing had worked.

I explained to her that Jesus healed people when He lived on earth and that He had commissioned and empowered His followers to do the same.

Being a guru of the Dalai Lama, she began to read excerpts of his writings, telling me how the Dalai Lama and Jesus were similar in their teachings. I pointed out that the difference was that the Dalai Lama could not heal her husband, but that Jesus could.

Finally, she closed her book of Dalai Lama passages and began to speak to her husband, who was now awake as the captain announced our arrival.

As we headed toward the baggage claim, the husband turned to me and said, "Hey, my wife told me that you are a healer. Do you think you could do your healing thing on me?"

Before I could think through the request, I responded, "Oh sure, no problem!" And then I felt like stuffing the words back into my mouth as I realized what I had just committed myself to.

Looking quite perplexed, the man asked, "Do we need to sit down or go somewhere to do this?"

"Oh, no," I responded. "I can do it as we're walking."

So, as we began to walk toward the baggage claim, I placed my hand on his arm and began to release God's presence. I said something like, "I release the goodness of God and His healing presence over your body. Cancer, I command you to leave this body. I release restoration of every cell in your body, until it conforms to the will of Heaven."

When we got to the baggage claim area a few minutes later, I asked how his arm felt. (He had been experiencing pain prior to my prayer.) He indicated that there was no change, but both he and his wife were visibly thankful that I had prayed. We hugged, and exchanged business cards—her card that read *"Massage therapist, yoga instructor, follower of the Dalai Lama,"* and my card, which read *"Bethel Church, pastor on staff."*

I left feeling good that I had broken through fear and stepped out to give God a chance to help these nice people who desperately needed a miracle. I remember praying that God would continue to reveal Himself to them.

The next week, one of our intercessors at Bethel Church came to me with a prophetic word that she said was from God. She explained that this prophetic word was so weird that she did not want to share it. After some encouragement, she finally relented and said, "The Lord wants you to know that the cabbage and tofu sandwich was from Him."

"How did you know that?" I quizzed with amazement.

"I was praying, and the Lord told me to tell you that," she replied, "Does that mean anything to you?"

"Are you kidding with me?" I shot back.

"No, are you kidding with me?"

Immediately I realized that God, in His mercy, was not calling me to start eating cabbage and tofu sandwiches, but rather, to further pursue this divine encounter that I had had with the Dalai Lama woman and her husband. I had a problem, however; after much searching, I could not find the business card the woman had given me.

Two weeks later, I was wearing the same shirt that I had been wearing on the day of the encounter on the airplane, and I found the card in my shirt pocket. I called the woman, who was very appreciative of my follow-up call. She related that, as soon as I had left the baggage claim at the airport, all of the pain in her husband's arm had left. Furthermore, he had just been back to the oncologist, who, after reexamining him, declared him to be totally clear of cancer. Previously he had gone through all sorts of therapies without success, but Jesus touched him through my hands, and the man was healed.

God Uses Ordinary People

Jesus has called every believer to live a naturally supernatural life. He has called each one of us to be a *healer*—to bring the Kingdom to earth so that what is in Heaven would be on the earth (see Matt. 6:9-10). Our mandate, then, is to represent Him on earth (see 2 Cor. 5:20). We are called to do what Jesus did, to demonstrate the Good News through a natural lifestyle of signs and wonders.

In Matthew 10:7-8, Jesus commanded *all* of His disciples to "Preach this message: 'The kingdom of heaven is near.' Heal the sick, raise the dead, cleanse those who have leprosy, drive out demons...." The command is still the same for us as it was for the first disciples. Each one of us, no matter how ordinary we may feel, is called to bring the Kingdom to earth in extraordinary ways.

Interestingly, Jesus did not look at John, the disciple of intimacy, and say, "Oh, I forgot, John, you are more of an introvert. I know that you much more prefer the 'secret place' of intimacy, where you can lay your head on my shoulder. I know that you are not an evangelist. Don't worry about going; I'll just send Peter. He's an extrovert. He'll say anything to anyone and take risk at every opportunity!" No, Jesus sent out all 12, regardless of personality, temperament, or gifting. He sent out the introvert with the extrovert, the timid with the bold, and the ungifted with the gifted to preach and demonstrate the Good News.

In the same way, God has called each one of us to live an extraordinarily supernatural life. In my own journey of developing a supernatural lifestyle, I have always felt intimidated and inadequate as I have ventured into new realms of risk. I have always been very conscious of my incompetency. I have also come to the conclusion that, if God can use *me* to do the extraordinary, then He can use anyone.

Throughout the Bible we find account after account of God using people who felt inadequate to do His will. For example, I can certainly relate to Gideon's feelings of inadequacy when God called him to lead the way in defeating a formidable enemy with just a few seemingly insufficient resources (see Judg. 6). I can certainly relate to his response to God's call to rise up and do something about the injustices that were being levied on the people of God. I have felt the same response rise up in me: "I'm the smallest. I'm the weakest. What can I do?"

I do a lot of traveling to churches all over the country, equipping, imparting, and activating believers to live a naturally supernatural lifestyle. It is so much fun to watch people who have never seen someone healed (or have never even prayed for someone's healing) see a healing happen for the first time. The comment most have is, "I can't believe that just happened through me."

The key to living a naturally supernatural life is to know that *ordinary* in the Kingdom is *extraordinary* on earth. The Kingdom of God is ordinarily extraordinary in itself, and this extraordinary Kingdom is within us (see Luke 17:21). Therefore, it should be normal that, when we release the Kingdom of God through our lives, extraordinary things begin to happen, like miracles, healings, prophetic insights into circumstances and people's lives, and deliverances of the oppressed.

God intends each believer to be a carrier of His extraordinary Kingdom, as the apostle Paul teaches in Colossians 1:27, "...[It is] Christ in you, the hope of glory." Therefore, we are called to live a naturally supernatural life because "Jesus is the same yesterday and today and forever" (Heb. 13:8).

JESUS WANTS TO GET OUT OF THE BOX

If you are a believer, Christ lives *in* you. It is also true that the Christ who lives *within* you wants to live *through* you. Jesus wants to get out of the box; He wants to reveal His glory through ordinary extraordinary people like you and me. In fact, you may be the only representation (re-presentation) of Jesus that some people ever see. You are their hope for encountering God's glory.

To this end, the Bible is clear, in Second Corinthians 5:20, when it says, "We are therefore Christ's ambassadors, as though God were making His appeal through us...."

In Isaiah 60:1-3, Isaiah commands us:

Arise, shine, for your light has come, and the glory of the Lord rises upon you. See, darkness covers the earth and thick darkness is over the peoples, but the Lord rises upon you and His glory appears over you. Nations will come to your light, and kings to the brightness of your dawn.

We are to reflect to the world the glory that is shining on us from God's presence. We are to reveal God's extraordinary goodness, as demonstrated in signs and wonders, miracles, healings, prophetic encouraging words, smiles, forgiveness, and practical acts of service to those around us. It is the kindness of God that leads to repentance (see Rom. 2:4). His kindness, reflected in His glory (released through us), attracts people to the good, kind, extraordinary God whom they see being demonstrated in an extraordinary way.

This same command is reiterated by Jesus in Matthew 5:14-16, as He points out:

You are the light of the world. A city on a hill cannot be hidden. Neither do people light a lamp and put it under a bowl. Instead they put it on its stand, and it gives light to everyone in the house. In the same way, let your light shine before men, that they may see your good deeds and praise your Father in heaven.

In other words, Jesus wants to shine through our lives; He wants out of the box. Christ in us has the answers that those around us are waiting for. Through Christ, we have access to every resource in Heaven that can meet every need represented here on earth.

Who, Me?

I heard a story of a woman who complained to God over and over about the terrible condition of the world. The Lord listened patiently to her laundry list of worldly woes. After she had finished, the Lord asked what she thought should be done about all of these problems. One by one, the woman listed solution after solution that would make the world a better place to live. After she was finished, the Lord promptly replied, "Those are fantastic ideas. I give you full authority to implement them." The woman responded in shock, "Who, me?"

Sadly, many people shy away from the supernatural gifts, thinking that they do not have the power to perform supernatural feats. The reality is that they don't. None of us have the power to heal, save, prophesy, or set people free; nevertheless, God has commissioned us to go and do these things—to make the world a better place to live.

In Acts 3, after Peter and John healed the cripple at the Gate Beautiful, the onlookers were obviously amazed at what they had just witnessed. There seemed to be an underlying sentiment among the crowd that there was something inherently super-special about Peter and John, that they were some kind of superheroes with special superhero power that made them unique. Peter, most likely recognizing this attitude, responded:

Men of Israel, why does this surprise you? Why do you stare at us as if by our own power or godliness we had made this man walk (Acts 3:12).

Then, after a short sermon, he adds:

By faith in the name of Jesus, this man whom you see and know was made strong. It is Jesus' name and the faith that comes through Him that has given this complete healing to him, as you can all see (Acts 3:16).

To say that *we have* the power to heal someone is inaccurate, but to say that *we do not have* the power to heal someone is equally inaccurate. We cannot heal anyone, but Christ in us can. We cannot set anyone free, but Christ in us can. We cannot save anyone from his or her sins, but Christ in us can.

Conversely, it is almost as if God will not heal, deliver, and save without us. Certainly God has the power to heal us on His own. But God, in His sovereignty, has chosen to partner with believers to bring His Kingdom rule to the earth, just as He did when He commissioned Adam in Genesis 1:28 to "fill the earth and subdue it." Obviously God had the power to rule the earth, but He chose to give the responsibility and authority to us.

In Matthew 10:8, Jesus told His disciples to give away what they had freely received. What had they freely received? "[Jesus]...gave them *authority* to drive out evil spirits and to heal every disease and sickness" (Matt. 10:1). In Matthew 28:18, Jesus said, "All authority in heaven and on earth has been given to Me," implying that He was giving His authority to the disciples so that they could represent and expand His Kingdom. Therefore, with authority comes inherent responsibility.

Many wonder why more people are not coming into the Kingdom. After all, we have the truth—the Good News! Maybe it is because we are waiting for others who are "gifted" to do what we have all been given responsibility and authority to do. If we could grasp the ramifications of the fact that we have already been commissioned and authorized to go represent the Kingdom, maybe we would have more confidence to release what is already inside of us. As a result, the world around us, in our sphere of influence, would be better off because His Kingdom would come.

WE ARE PHYSICIAN'S ASSISTANTS

My son, Chad, and I were taken to a hospital recently to pray for a woman who was very ill. On the way to her room, I noticed the Emergency Room waiting area filled with people needing attention. I told my son and the local pastor who had invited us that the Emergency Room is where we should really go since those waiting were a captive audience and in obvious need.

On the way out, after praying for the woman, I asked the pastor to wait while I took a detour into the Emergency Room waiting area. Entering, I noticed several people who looked like they desperately needed to see a doctor. Immediately, I announced the good news, "If anyone does not want to wait for the doctor, I can take care of you now."

You see, wherever I go, I think of myself as a physician's assistant. I assist the Great Physician in bringing the Kingdom wherever I find a need that demands the Kingdom coming.

Oddly enough, however, when I asked if anyone needed healing, they all just shook their heads. "Well, that's strange," I replied, "because I felt like God wanted to heal someone's knee."

Still, they shook their heads in denial until the son of an elderly man piped up and said, "Wait a minute, Dad, your knee is so messed up that you have to wear a brace and can barely walk!" The man reluctantly pulled up his pant leg, revealing a brace that extended from the middle of his thigh to the middle of his calf.

I asked if he would like me to take care of his knee, but to my surprise, he shook his head and said, "Oh, no thanks, I'm OK," to which I responded, "How can you be all right when you can barely walk?" Without hesitation, I began to wave my hand toward him as I said, "God, release Your goodness on this man. Just be healed in Jesus' name."

Immediately, the man invited me to come closer (he was apparently sensing God's presence) and then enthusiastically asked me to place my hand on his knee. After I prayed for a short time, he showed signs of improvement. He started moving his leg around and flexing his knee with a look of astonishment.

Meanwhile, his daughter began motioning to her neck and shoulder and asked if I could also help her because she had been in a recent car accident and had been in pain and lacked mobility ever since. With the elderly father now healed, I moved over to release God's healing presence on his daughter, and in less than two minutes, all of the pain left and she had complete mobility.

During this time, my son, Chad, also spoke out a word of knowledge for someone with back pain, which turned out to be for another family member of the elderly man. After Chad prayed for a few minutes, the man started bending down at the waist, proving he had been completely healed.

As I walked toward the exit of the Emergency Room, I had to walk past the elderly man whose knee had just been healed. As I started to pass by, he reached out, grabbed my hand, and pulled it down to touch his other knee, which also needed healing. As my hand touched his knee, he was instantly healed!

OUR FATHER IS ALWAYS HEALING

In John 5:19, we are told that Jesus could only do what He saw His Father doing because whatever the Father did the Son also did. For a long time, I thought that Jesus would stop in the midst of daily activities and normal encounters with people, and ask, "Father, what are You doing here?" In other words, "Do You want to heal this person? Do You want Me to prophesy to this person? Do You want Me to help this person?" It's almost as though I thought that Jesus did not release the Kingdom unless He got a green light from the Father.

I want to propose that the Father has already given us a green light to release the Kingdom to anyone, wherever we go. I am reminded of the woman who had an issue of blood who touched the hem of Jesus' robe in

Luke 8. Jesus didn't stop and say, "Hold it, woman, we need to ask the Father whether or not He wants to do this right now." No, the woman touched His clothing and drew out the power resident within Him through faith. She didn't ask; she just grabbed what was already available in Jesus.

At the same time, Jesus only did what the Father was doing. So, the question is whether this is manifested on a case-by-case basis or as an ongoing lifestyle. The fact is that our Father in Heaven is always healing, and we know this because one of His names is *Yahweh Rapha*—"the Lord who heals you" (see Exod. 15:26). This reflects His nature, character, attributes, actions, and will. The Father's name never changes, so His will never changes.

The Father does not sit in Heaven thinking, "All right, I'm healing...*you*...*you*...and *you*...but not *you*." No, God's nature, His will, is to heal everyone. He is always releasing healing virtue from Heaven. It is up to us to administrate it on earth. Jesus healed wherever He went because He saw His Father always healing from Heaven.

Jesus did not have special times in which He healed people, prophesied, or set them free. It wasn't like He had a healing conference where people would sign up for the chance to be touched. No, He walked through a crowd, and a woman with a blood issue came into contact with Him and she was healed (see Luke 8:43-48). It was that natural. We also read of people being healed as Peter's shadow covered them because he carried the same Kingdom presence as Jesus (see Acts 5:14-16).

Jesus lived a supernatural lifestyle. He was naturally supernatural because, "God anointed Jesus of Nazareth with the Holy Spirit and power...because God was with Him" (Acts 10:38). We have the same anointing that Jesus received because we have received the same Holy Spirit, who continues to anoint and empower believers today. Therefore, we have the same obligation to do only what the Father is doing today—just as He was doing in Jesus' time on earth.

NICE PEOPLE IN CASINOS

Sometimes we get the idea that Jesus only heals in church on a Sunday morning or at a special "revival" meeting. But God wants to heal people wherever we go. Once I was driving through Reno, Nevada, with a team of our Bethel School of Supernatural Ministry students. We decided to stop off at one of the casinos to take advantage of their all-you-can-eat buffet. The food is amazing and cheap!

While I was in line to get my made-to-order stir-fry, a man came limping up alongside of me on a crutch, carrying his plateful of delectable goodies for the chef to cook up on the open grill. I noticed that the man had a leg brace on and asked what had caused his apparent injury. He pointed in the direction of the mountains and simply said, "Skiing." After a few more questions, I found out that he had torn a ligament in his knee and could barely walk on it with a crutch, let alone bend it in any way.

Without hesitation, I asked if he would like me to heal his knee. I told him that I had seen many knees healed as I released God's goodness and that I could do the same for him. He agreed, so I bent down with my free hand, briefly touched his knee, said a simple statement about God's Kingdom coming, and declared that there are no injured knees in Heaven and that there shouldn't be any here either.

Later, while I was at the dessert center with one of my students, the man I had prayed for came walking by holding his crutch and knee brace under his arm.

"What happened to you?" I asked.

"While I was eating, I felt my knee continually improving, so I stood up and found that I could put my full weight on it without any pain. I started moving it around and found that I had full mobility, so I took the knee brace off, and my knee felt brand-new. I think I might even go dancing tonight." And then he added, as if to give a postscript to his testimony, "Boy, there sure are nice people in this casino."

Perhaps because of a lack of teaching, many people do not see a lot of people healed simply because they do not pray for people; they do not think they have what it takes to be a physician's assistant. As a result, opportunity after opportunity to demonstrate God's Kingdom passes them by. I want to encourage you that you *can* live a naturally supernatural life and do extraordinary feats as an ordinary Christian. In the following chapters, we will look at different Kingdom keys that unlock these possibilities.

Chapter 2

PRAYERS THAT
UNLOCK HEAVEN

WE are all called to release God's Kingdom here on earth. Each one of us has been placed in a sphere of influence in which we have been given responsibility to release the Good News. All of us have been called as revivalists to impact the world around us as we release God's manifest presence in practical, naturally supernatural ways.

Wherever Jesus went, He preached the Good News of the Kingdom, demonstrating the Kingdom with supernatural actions. In Matthew 4:23, we are told, "Jesus went throughout Galilee, teaching in their synagogues, preaching the good news of the kingdom, and healing every disease and sickness among the people." Jesus lived a naturally supernatural life.

The disciples were called to the same lifestyle as Jesus. As pointed out in the previous chapter, Jesus had called them to be "fishers of men" (Matt. 4:19). In other words, He was training them to be world-changers who would do the same things that He had been modeling to them, who would live naturally supernatural lives.

Leading up to Matthew 6, the disciples were probably wondering how they were going to follow in Jesus' footsteps. They may have been asking themselves, "How are we going to be able to release God's Kingdom the way Jesus is doing it?"

I am sure most of the disciples were feeling at least a little incompetent and unconfident in that regard. Most likely, those feelings of inadequacy prompted the request that is implied in Matthew 6 and recorded in Luke 11:1: "Teach us to pray." The disciples were well aware that, when Jesus prayed, good things happened. It was obvious that He had favor with God, which enabled Him to influence Heaven to come to earth through His prayers. They needed the secret to living a naturally supernatural life.

The disciples had never seen miracles of the scope and frequency with which Jesus did them. Furthermore, they probably were not used to having their prayers answered, especially to the extent that Jesus' were. Yet, interestingly enough, it was in the context of the disciples watching Him perform miracles and feeling inadequate in mirroring them that Jesus taught His disciples how to pray.

MOVING HEAVEN TO EARTH

Of course, there are different types of prayer that can be utilized by the believer. There is listening prayer, in which we receive instruction, wisdom, encouragement, or comfort. There is soaking prayer, in which we are continually filled with God's presence. And there are various forms of celebratory prayers of thanksgiving for what God has done. All of these forms of prayer, as well as others, have specific value, although they are not the forms that Jesus taught His disciples to pray here in Matthew 6.

In Matthew 6:9-10, Jesus instructed His disciples to pray, "Our Father in heaven, hallowed be Your name, Your Kingdom come, Your will be done on earth as it is in heaven." Jesus was teaching them how to influence

Heaven to come to earth. He was teaching them how to petition God to release His Kingdom, bringing intervention in the affairs of man.

The goal of petition prayer is to change something, to move something, to influence God to intervene where man cannot. It is asking God for miracle breakthrough where there is no hope. It is causing Heaven to invade earth so that His Kingdom comes, so that His will is done on earth as it is in Heaven.

Jesus was teaching His disciples how to move Heaven to meet our daily needs, "Give us today our daily bread" (Matt. 6:11), whether for nutritional sustenance, emotional fortitude or comfort, spiritual renewal, miraculous intervention in circumstances, or physical healing. He was instructing them to influence Heaven to bring relational reconciliation, "Forgive us our debts, as we also have forgiven our debtors" (Matt. 6:12). He was teaching them to bring Heaven to earth in order to overcome the powers of the evil one, "...deliver us from the evil one" (Matt. 6:13).

In a sense, all religions of the world attempt to influence their god(s) to intervene on their behalf. I just spent two weeks ministering in India, where hundreds of gods are worshiped for protection, provision, healing, and every other need known to people.

On one occasion, we went to a place where about 30 million men make a pilgrimage each year during a two-week window, crawling on their stomachs, cutting themselves, and chanting prescribed mantras in hopes of influencing six rocks, which are stationed on top of a hill, to bless them with their supposed supernatural powers.

Year after year, they make the same journey to worship these rocks with the same unanswered results, yet they continue in their futile petitions, hoping for a breakthrough. It is like the definition of insanity that I have heard, "Doing the same failing thing over and over, expecting different results."

It is in this context that Jesus said, "...Do not keep on babbling like pagans, for they think they will be heard because of their many words" (Matt. 6:7). Effectiveness of prayer for the pagans, then, is to pray the right words for a long time. But prayers based on length and repetition are not the key to releasing God's Kingdom.

Jesus also warns His disciples to not pray like the hypocrites, referring most likely to the religious leaders of the day who would pray for show (see Matt. 6:5). Eloquence and outward devotion are equally as ineffective in influencing God to intervene for our needs and desires. Religious prayers are not the answer to changing the world.

In the days of Jesus, the Jewish religious leaders had come up with several prayers that they were sure would influence God to bless them. These prayers had to be memorized and spoken with perfect accuracy in order to be effective. They were the formula to move Heaven to earth.

For example, the *Shema* (found in Deuteronomy 6:4-9), had to be quoted out loud two times a day to ensure God's blessing. The *Amidah,* also known as the *Eighteen Blessings,* was to be quoted word-for-word once a day. When printed out on 8½ x 11-inch paper, the *Amidah* covers seven pages!

Then there were the various forms of the *Kaddish*, which were written prayers that, when recited properly, were to release specific blessings for every occasion and need in life. There was the *Sabbath Kaddish*, the *Passover Kaddish*, a *Wedding Kaddish*, and a *Funeral Kaddish*, just to mention a few. The Jewish repertoire of religious prayers covered every base to ensure that God would move Heaven to earth for them.

The point that Jesus was making to His disciples in Matthew 6 was that the kind of prayer that influences God is not about whipping up the right words, the proper formula, or the perfect technique. Living a naturally supernatural life, releasing God's Kingdom, moving Heaven to earth, is a result of living in dynamic, intimate relationship with God.

"Speak to the Rock"

Moses provides a great example of one who lost this perspective. God had given him a staff to use as a tool to bring Heaven to earth. It was a symbol of the authority that God had given to him, and he used it to prove that God was with him as well as to provide for and protect the children of Israel. Each time Moses raised the staff as an authorized representative of the Kingdom on earth, Heaven would be unleashed to meet whatever need the Israelites had.

When Israel came to Rephidim, a deserted place with no water for the people to drink (see Exod. 17), they began to complain and quarrel with Moses, demanding that he give them something to drink. In verse 4, we are told that "Moses cried out to the Lord." In verse 6, God told him, "...Strike the rock, and water will come out of it for the people to drink." Moses struck the rock with the staff, and the people were able to drink the water that came from the rock.

Later the Israelites came to the desert of Zin and stopped to camp at Kadesh, where there was no water (see Num. 20). Once again, the people quarreled with Moses, demanding that he provide water. In verse 6, we are told, "Moses and Aaron went from the assembly to the entrance to the Tent of Meeting, and fell facedown, and the glory of the Lord appeared to them."

In the next verse, God told Moses to take the staff with him, but instead of striking the rock with the staff, God told Moses to "speak to the rock." But instead, in verse 11, Moses struck the rock twice, and water gushed out to provide for the people. Unfortunately, because of Moses' disobedience, he was not able to enter the Promised Land (see Num. 20:12).

Moses came to rely on his rod of religion more than on his relationship with God. He trusted in a proven formula and technique rather than in the "now" word of God. We must be careful not to let our breakthroughs of yesterday become religious forms today. We must remember that the authority that we have to release the Kingdom of God comes through intimate, personal relationship with God in the secret place rather than through a structure, formula, or technique.

DADDY, KISS IT...MAKE IT GO AWAY

I was walking into a conference that we were holding at our church when I heard my name being yelled out by a woman who was absolutely hysterical. She had a cell phone to her ear, trying to talk to a hospital dispatcher about getting an ambulance sent to the church, while at the same time desperately trying to get me to come over to where she was standing.

As it turned out, her 20-year-old son had just fallen while skateboarding 20 miles per hour down a hill near our church building. When I arrived, he was leaning against the wall next to her, unable to move, and shaking with shock. Tears welled up in his eyes, and it was obvious that he was in a great deal of pain. He indicated through clinched teeth that his hip felt like it had been severely crushed by the impact of the pavement and that he could not put any weight on it. It certainly looked like he needed to go to the hospital.

Meanwhile, his mother was still hysterically screaming into the cell phone, trying to get the ambulance moving, but she could not tell the dispatcher where to go because she did not know the address of the church. Someone was trying to give her the address, but because of the shock of seeing her son in such pain, she could not seem to focus.

I decided to turn my focus completely toward her son, who needed immediate attention. At that moment, I had a vision of a little boy coming to his father, crying, "Daddy, Daddy, I got an *owey*; kiss it and make it better." Then I saw the father bend down to kiss the injury, taking away all of the pain so that the boy was smiling with delight.

Immediately I knew that this was a picture of what Father God wanted to do for the young man standing before me. After explaining the vision I had just had, I knelt down in front of him, kissed my hand, and placed it on his injured hip.

An amazed expression came over his face, and he described a sensation of fire consuming his hip. Ten seconds later, all of the pain was gone, and he began to run up and down the hallway completely healed.

Meanwhile, his mother, who had just completed giving the ambulance dispatcher the needed address, matter-of-factly said that they were no longer needed and snapped the cell phone shut as she looked on in total astonishment.

A week later, I was asked to pray for a visiting pastor who had stomach cancer. He was in the fourth stage, with his stomach very distended. About a dozen of his leaders had come with him for moral support and were aligned in a semi-circle around him.

After hearing about his losing battle with the cancer, I remembered the vision that I had with the young man whose hip was healed in the hallway. I thought to myself, *I'll just kiss it and make it better.*

After giving the testimony, I asked the pastor if it would be all right if I kissed his stomach to release God's healing presence. He readily agreed and promptly lifted up his shirt, revealing his bulging, sweat-drenched, hairy stomach. This time I thought, *I'm going to literally kiss his stomach, because this is life and death; he needs a great miracle!*

So, in similar fashion to what I had done in the hallway a week prior, I knelt down and put my lips to the man's stomach and gave him a juicy, wet kiss!

This had better work, I thought to myself, *because this is about the most embarrassing thing I can imagine.*

Getting up, I was sure that God had honored my utilization of the appropriate key to unlock the power of Heaven and my willingness to go the extra distance to make sure the prayer was effective.

But then... *Nothing!* The pastor sheepishly, with embarrassment for me, reported that he did not feel any different. I then advised him to go to someone else who would listen for the current word of the Lord because it was certainly God's heart to bring Heaven to earth for him.

I learned a great lesson that day: effective, influential prayer is not about finding some secret code or applying the correct combination. It is not about wielding the staff of our proven strategies and structures. Rather, it is our dynamic relationship with God that motivates Him to move Heaven to earth.

WHO'S YOUR DADDY?

Effective prayer that brings Heaven to earth is about intimacy not performance, resting not striving, faith not formula, relationship not religion. Jesus taught His disciples that influencing Heaven to come to earth, so that His will is done, flows from intimacy of relationship in knowing God as "our Father." Understanding God as "our Father" is a primary key to living a naturally supernatural life.

Therefore, Jesus instructed His disciples to pray in the secret place to "our Father" (Matt. 6:6). There is a noticeable difference between the

Jewish religious prayers and the prayer model that Jesus taught the disciples. The Jews always addressed God as *"the Father"* in the *Amidah* and *Kaddish* (both of which, by the way, are very similar to the prayer here in Matthew 6), while Jesus practiced and taught His disciples to address God as *"our Father."*

The thought of addressing God as "our Father" was a huge deal in Jewish religious culture. For the Jew, saying that God was your father was considered blasphemous. That is why, in John 5:18, the religious leaders wanted to kill Jesus: "...He was even calling God His own Father, making Himself equal with God."

To the Jews, God was the Father of all creation; He was the originator of man and everything else in the world. God was, therefore, considered "the Father," signifying a transcendent relationship between God and man. To say that God was your own personal Father meant that you were not of human origin, but, in fact, God.

On the other hand, Abraham was considered the father of the Jews. He was the originator of Israel; it is similar to the way that we refer to George Washington as one of the founding fathers of America (since he helped to originate the United States). Likewise, Adam, the first man, was the father of humankind. Therefore, we are considered children of humanity, children of America, or, for the Jew, children of Abraham; all of these speak of human origins.

Jesus, however, had no hesitation in calling God His own father; He knew who His Daddy was. Jesus called God His own Father, which was to say that He was of divine origin and, therefore, not of this world.

In John 1:13, we are told that we are "children born not of natural descent, nor of human decision or a husband's will, but born of God." Thus, like Jesus, we are now of a divine origin; we are literally God's children, and we have all of the rights and privileges that go along with that status.

So it was with that understanding that Jesus taught His disciples to pray "our Father," "my Father." Moreover, when we know God as "our Father" (versus "the Father"), then we will know who we are as His children, and we will begin to understand our identity.

It is out of our identity that we have access. It is out of access that we have intimacy. It is out of intimacy that we can release through authority what we have accessed. And our authority results in influence—"Your kingdom come, Your will be done..." (Matt. 6:10). This all begins in knowing God as "our Father."

Otherwise, we will only relate to Him as a servant relates to his master, and servants do not have the same privileges as sons and daughters. In John 15:15, Jesus said, "I no longer call you servants.... I have called you friends...." In First John 3:1, John gives a greater revelation when he points out that we are the children of God. The apostle Paul confirms this reality in Romans 8:16 when he says, "The Spirit Himself testifies with our spirit that we are God's children." Furthermore, in Galatians 4:1-7, Paul speaks of the inheritance that we have as children and says that we do not have to wait to access it because Jesus has already died.

CHILDREN GET TO RAID THE REFRIGERATOR

Children have greater access to the Father's house than servants do. When our son, Chad, first got married, it seemed like my wife, Theresa, and I saw more of him then than we had in the previous three years when he lived with us full time. His wife worked during the evenings as a server in a restaurant, which meant that he had most of his evenings free.

Sometimes, I would come out of my room at night and find that my son had welcomed himself into the house without any kind of warning. He would not call. He would not even knock to let us know that he had arrived.

He just walked right in unannounced! You see, sons do not have to make reservations to come into their father's house. Sons have continual access.

I would usually find him at the refrigerator, looking for a leftover barbequed New York steak that I had hidden in the back for safe keeping. Inevitably, he would find my treasured lunch for the next day and have no shame whatsoever about eating it with joy in his heart! Why? It is because he is a son, and sons have access to the father's house and the refrigerator.

As a father, I would not even think about getting angry over my son coming into my house unannounced and raiding my refrigerator. I actually enjoy watching my son be blessed, and I have plenty of resources to get more steak. I love that my son wishes to come to my house when he wants to eat and hang out, swim in the pool, or watch my big-screen HD television.

On the other hand, if the carpet cleaners showed up at seven o'clock in the morning, unannounced, and let themselves into the house to start cleaning my carpets without an appointment, I would be very upset. My anger would only increase if one of the employees had scoped out one of my perfectly barbequed, leftover New York steaks and was eating it with glee! I would tell them to get out, to call to make an appointment when it was convenient for me, and to never think about touching my steak because they are servants, not sons.

Sons can come into their heavenly Father's house at any time, while servants can only access God's presence on Sundays and Wednesdays. Sons can raid their heavenly Father's refrigerator any time they want, taking anything they want, while servants only get what is handed to them as pay for the work they do. Sons have access because of their identity, while servants gain access through works.

While I was ministering in Tepic, Mexico, a young woman who had been in a car accident came to me the last night. Her jawbone had been so badly crushed, into so many pieces, that the doctor had to remove it, leaving her without a jawbone. She could not smile or bite down on an apple because she had no strength. Because of the missing bone structure, her face fell limp on one side.

As I prayed for her, I thought, *Well, I'll just have to grab a new jawbone from Heaven.* In my spirit, I reached up into God's resources of "spare parts" and released a new jawbone into her mouth. Although she felt heat and a tingling sensation, nothing else seemed to happen.

The next year when I returned, however, a smiling young woman came to me right away and told me that she had been eating apples for the past year, ever since I had prayed for her. She went on to tell me the whole story. On the way home after I had prayed for her, she began to feel the bone growing back, and by the next morning, she had a new jawbone! She went back to her doctor, who did not believe that it was her until he took X-rays and compared them. He declared, "I am an atheist, but this is a miracle!"

In Luke 12:32, Jesus declared, "...Your Father has been pleased to give you the kingdom." If we could just grasp the significance of our identity, we would have increased confidence in accessing and releasing what is available in our Father's house.

CHILDREN GET TO SNUGGLE

Part of Jesus' effectiveness in releasing the Kingdom wherever He went was tied to the intimate times that He had with His Father. Throughout the Gospels, we read of Jesus spending time alone with Father God. He spent time in the secret place where He could be intimate with His Father.

In John 14:10-11, Jesus said:

...It is the Father, living in Me [intimacy], *who is doing His work. Believe Me when I say that I am in the Father and the Father is in Me; or at least believe on the evidence of the miracles themselves.*

It was out of that place of intimacy that He was able to influence God to move Heaven to earth; it was out of intimacy that He lived a naturally supernatural life.

Prayer that influences God comes out of intimacy, not formulaic or long-winded prayers. That is why Jesus taught His disciples to pray in secret (see Matt. 6:6). Not only was He instructing them to pray in a place without public fanfare, unlike the hypocrites, but also to pray in secret where there would be the possibility for intimacy with their heavenly Father. Prayer that influences Heaven toward earth comes through intimacy.

Often my daughter, Alexa, likes to lie down on the couch while we are watching a movie together and put her feet on my lap. I love having her feet in my face, even if they are stinky, because we are snuggling. My son will sometimes wrap his arm over me and put his leg over mine (while eating potato chips and dropping crumbs all over me) as we watch a basketball game on television. I love it because we are snuggling.

Children get to snuggle with their father; servants do not get to snuggle. If the carpet cleaner came into my television room, sat down, wrapped his arm around me, swung his leg over mine, and put his head on my chest for some snuggle time, I would have to resort to some made-up karate moves to get him off of me. Why? It is because he is a servant, not a son. Only children get to snuggle.

The reason intimacy is so important is that the power to release signs and wonders, miracles, and healings comes out of the presence of God. In a sense, living a naturally supernatural life is as simple as soaking and leaking; we are like a sponge, soaking up His presence, and when we walk through the world, we leak what we have received.

I learned this lesson several years ago, by myself, as I was simply resting in my Father's presence. For years I had been debilitated by a 14-millimeter herniation of my L4, L5 disc. For about 16 years, I had to walk around with ice packs tucked in my pants and sleep with pillows between and under my knees just to stay comfortable for a few hours at a time.

But on one occasion, I was ministering with our Bethel School of Supernatural Ministry students at a church in Southern California, and after the ministry time, another leader and I were "whacked" by the Spirit and sprawled out on the floor, encountering Daddy's love.

After about an hour in this "secret place," I realized that I had been lying on the hard floor of the stage without any pain in my lower back. In fact, it felt like I was floating on a cloud of light about two feet off the ground, even though I was conscious of the fact that I was not actually doing that in the natural. When I decided to sit up several minutes later, I found that I had absolutely no pain. I was completely healed, and I had not even asked for it! Five years later, I am still running, playing basketball, skiing, and sleeping without any discomfort.

Our heavenly Father wants to snuggle with us. He wants to be intimate with us in the secret place of His presence. In order for us to have the confidence to come into His presence, we must know who we are; we must know our identity as sons and daughters of our heavenly Father.

Jesus Himself did not begin His ministry on earth until He first heard, "This is My son…" at His baptism (Matt. 3:17). It was as He heard those words that He also knew that God was His Father. Each one of us must have a personal encounter in which we hear for ourselves that God is "our Father."

In John 14:8, Philip said to Jesus, "Show us the Father." And right now, I would like to invite you to close your eyes and ask Father God to reveal Himself to you so that you can hear for yourself, "This is My son," "This is

My daughter." For it is only as we know God as "our Father" that we can also confidently pray "Your Kingdom come..."—the prayer that unlocks Heaven!

Chapter 3

"YADA, YADA, YADA"

MANY are familiar with the phrase "yada, yada, yada," made popular by the longtime sitcom, *Seinfeld*. In the context of the show, the catchy phrase is used to imply, "OK, enough already, get on with it, get to the point, I know already," and is usually said with one's head tilted back and eyes rolling up for dramatic effect. It refers to people being redundant, monotonous, or verbose. It is also used as a *fill-in-the-blank phrase* for details that are either unimportant or obvious to everyone. That is how most of us have come to know the term *yada*.

The word *yada* is found throughout the Old Testament, although it has a much more significant meaning than is depicted on *Seinfeld*. In Genesis 4:1, we are told, "Adam lay [*yada*] with his wife Eve, and she became pregnant and gave birth to Cain...." In some Bible translations (such as the NKJV), *yada* is translated "knew," while in others (like the NIV quoted here) it is translated "lay."

Both translations are correct, but there is more to this word, *yada*, than even these two translations depict. *Yada* means "to know" in five distinct dimensions. Moreover, all five aspects or dimensions combined are essential to comprehending the full meaning of *yada*. The Greek word *ginosko* in the

New Testament has a very similar interpretive connotation to *yada*, and it is used in place of *yada* in the Old Testament Greek Septuagint version.[1]

Understanding the complete ramification of the meaning of *yada* is vital in learning how to unlock Heaven and live a naturally supernatural life. Jesus lived in *yada* relationship with His Father, which fueled His ability to release Heaven to earth as demonstrated in the signs and wonders, miracles, and healings that He accomplished.

Similarly, if we want to do the things that Jesus did, we must also live in *yada* relationship with God. With that in mind, we will look at each dimension of meaning for *yada/ginosko* and apply it to living a naturally supernatural life.

WHERE'S WALDO

The first dimension of *yada* is to *know* something or someone in complete detail. It means to study, analyze, or investigate something until you *know* something or someone completely. It is to *know* something like a detective would seek to *know* the details of a mystery. *Yada* is to know God in increasing detail.[2]

Knowing more of God has been my lifelong goal. I believe that should be the goal of any growing relationship. My wife and I have been married over 30 years, and while we know each other extensively, we are still finding out more about each other; we are growing in our *yada*.

How much more of God is there to know? How many of us have a complete revelation of His nature, personality, attributes, and ways? How much have we actually experienced of what we know intellectually? In reality, no matter how much we already know and have experienced of God, there is always more because He is infinite.

In Ephesians 1:17, the apostle Paul prays that the Ephesian believers would have a "spirit of wisdom and revelation, so that you may *know* [*ginosko*] Him better." In other words, they needed more detail in order to know (*yada/ginosko*) God better. Furthermore, even though they already *knew* God, there was still more to *know*. Therefore, they needed increased revelation; they needed repeated "Waldo encounters."

When my son was growing up, the *Where's Waldo* books were very popular. Of course, the object of the book was to find Waldo cleverly hidden throughout the pages of crowds of people. Invariably, my son would bring his new book to me, asking me to find Waldo.

There were times when I would look up and down, side to side, diagonally, and by section for several minutes at a time, unable to find Waldo. I would even feel a sense of accomplishment as I confidently proclaimed that "they" had forgotten to put Waldo in the crowd on that particular page.

Inevitably, after my unsuccessful search, my son would point and excitedly exclaim, "There's Waldo! There's Waldo!" Immediately, Waldo became 4 feet by 4 feet on the page to me. I had received a revelation! Amazingly, from that time forth, every time I turned to the page where I had discovered Waldo, I could immediately point him out as though I had known where he was my whole life.

"Waldo encounters" are times when truth jumps out at us as revelation, when what was previously hidden becomes apparent and even obvious. For example, how many of us have read the same portion of Scripture over and over for years, and then, one day, we have a truth jump out at us that we had never seen there before? I call those "Waldo encounters."

We find Waldo encounters all throughout Church history—revelations that are given to the Church to increase its ability to know God better. During these Waldo encounters, those who could not find Waldo in the picture, so to speak, often persecuted those who discovered hidden truths about God's nature, personality, and will. Ironically, the very groups that persecuted those who had breakthroughs often accepted these same revelations as basic truths eventually. It is also interesting to note that some individuals or groups who were persecuted during their Waldo encounter later persecuted others who were experiencing the next Waldo encounter. For example, when the Anabaptists had the revelation that water baptism should come after a confession of Christ, they were persecuted by the Lutherans, who held that infant baptism was sufficient. Then later, the Anabaptists persecuted the Pentecostals when they had a revelation of the baptism of the Holy Spirit evidenced by speaking in tongues.

God always wants to reveal more of Himself to us so that we can know more of Him.

THE MONZA

The second dimension of *yada* is to *know* something or someone from a technical perspective. It is to know how something or someone works technically in all aspects.[3] This dimension of *yada* is part of the *wisdom* that Paul was praying for in Ephesians 1:17.

So then, *yada* does not just know what elements comprise something or someone, but also *how* that person or thing works. Wisdom, in this context, knows how God and His Kingdom operate—how God works in releasing power on earth for signs and wonders and miracles.

During our first ministry staff position, in 1982, we were given a Chevrolet Monza with low mileage. What we did not know about the car at the time was that this model had been discontinued because of a problem with the aluminum block engine, which would expand under heat and cause major oil loss. After we had the car for a month, the engine blew up.

The rest of the car was in pretty good shape, and we did not have the finances available for a new car, so I decided to save some money and fix the engine myself. I figured that, since I had a college degree, even though it was in biblical studies, I should be able to follow the directions in the manual step-by-step with no problems, despite the fact that I had no previous experience working on cars.

In all of my wisdom, I decided to take off each part of the engine and place them in chronological order on the single shelf that I had tacked up around my one-car garage. I figured that I would simply put all of the parts back in from the opposite side of the garage once I had finished dismantling the engine—how hard could it be?

Well, after I almost blew my head off, singeing my eyebrow hair and the top of my head, because I had pulled off the air-conditioner hose full of compressed anti-freeze, the unthinkable happened. When I had most of the engine parts lining the garage, the cumulative weight caused the shelving to collapse, sending all of the parts in a heap to the floor. It looked like a game of "pick-up sticks," all of the parts intermingled in disarray.

By the time I got the engine back in, I had brackets, bolts, and parts left over that I could not recognize or fit into the engine. So I just left them out or bent them to fit. To my surprise, the car would not start. Over and over I tried, but to no avail. I even tried prayer, and later, a swift kick; nothing worked.

As a last resort, I called a mechanic friend of mine to come over and help. After five minutes, he just shook his head and said, "Kevin, you have completely destroyed this engine. I'm going to have to redo everything!" Apparently, those missing bolts, brackets, and spare parts were necessary components in a fully functional engine! By the time he finished rebuilding and replacing the engine, it cost almost twice as much as it would have if I had just taken the car to a certified mechanic in the first place!

How many of us have attempted to release the Kingdom by following the manual (a particular Scripture or someone's ten-steps to success), only to end up with a heap of confusion and frustration on the floor as we try to figure out why the "project" did not start? I found out that there is a difference between knowing the names of the parts and knowing how they work.

Similarly, we could save ourselves a lot of time and heartache if we understood the underlying principles of how God and His Kingdom operate. The apostle Paul prayed that the Ephesians would have a *Spirit of wisdom* so that they would *know* Him in applied technical expertise.

Through the years, I have had many frustrating occasions while attempting to get breakthrough for someone's physical healing. During those times, I prayed every Scripture related to the promise of healing, mustered up all of my mustard-seed-sized faith, and used up all of my creative ideas for how to unlock Heaven. Now I have learned to relax with the expert (God) in *yada time*, during which I get needed downloads of wisdom on how to help someone get a breakthrough.

Yada means understanding God's ways so that we can take from Him what we need, as well as putting back into Him the things that He desires from us to further our relationship. *Yada* is not just knowing the details about God, but also knowing His ways, as Moses prayed in Exodus 33:13: "If You are pleased with me, teach me Your ways so I may know [*yada*] You and continue to find favor with You...."

How many of us actually *know* God so well that we know the intricacies of how He operates—the keys that unlock His presence in and through our lives?

Who Wants to Go to Hawaii With Me?

The third dimension of *yada* is knowing God through personal experience.[4] A lot of people know *about* God, but God wants us to know Him through encounters in which we personally experience His presence. There is a big difference between knowing something in theory, in virtual reality, and knowing something through personal experience.

For example, imagine that I offered to take you to Hawaii on a two-week, all-expense-paid vacation. Wouldn't you start to get a little excited thinking about the white, sandy beaches, the coconut aroma on the tropical breezes, and the mesmerizing waves lapping toward your lounge chair as you nap your way through the afternoon? How many of you are ready to go right now?

Would you still want to go if I told you that I was going to be flying the plane? How about if I told you that I had never actually flown a plane but that I had read the manual and knew everything there is to know about flying? Would you be comforted if I assured you that I had passed all of the written tests and that, while I had never actually flown a real plane, I had successfully taken off and landed the last ten attempts in the flight simulator? Would you still be excited about going to Hawaii with me?

If you answered "yes" to that question, then you are crazy! You should never fly with a pilot who has never actually flown a plane! It does not matter how much they have learned out of the book and in the flight simulator when it comes to flying a plane in real life.

When I was in seminary, I wrote a 30-page paper on the lineage of faith healing in America. I received an "A" on the paper, and I even received some encouragement about publishing it because of the extensive research that I had compiled. I was an expert on the history of faith healing in America, but I did not know how to heal the sick, and I never prayed for the sick!

At some point, our theology must lead to a theophany (*theo* means "God," *phaneo* means "an appearance of"), a God-appearance in which we encounter His presence. Our information must lead to revelation, a personal encounter that paves the way for transformation and produces manifestation (fruit).

In John 8:32, Jesus promised, "You will *know* [*yada/ginosko*] the truth, and the truth will set you free." Jesus was not suggesting that His followers become more educated with more information and head knowledge. No, He was pointing them toward personal encounters with God, the truth. It is not just knowing *about* the truth that sets us free; it is knowing (*yada/ginosko*) the truth; having experiential knowledge will set us free.

Jesus chastised the religious people of His day with these words:

> *You diligently study the Scriptures because you think that by them you possess eternal life. These are the Scriptures that testify about Me, yet you refuse to come to Me to have life* (John 5:39-40).

The Jewish Pharisees had made the mistake of confusing information with revelation, theory with practical experience, and study with encounter. The objective of studying the Scriptures is to lead us into relationship with God. Life is found in personal experience with Jesus, not in winning at Bible Trivial Pursuit.

God wants us to *have* an encounter so that we *become* an encounter so that *others* can have an encounter. *Yada* is experiencing a personal encounter with God so that we become a habitation of His presence and then "leak" His presence to others around us through signs and wonders, miracles, healings, and prophetic insights from His heart. In this way, they too can have a personal encounter with His presence.

FACE OFF

The fourth dimension of *yada* is to have a face-to-face encounter.[5] *Yada* means knowing something or someone up close and personal. A lot of people know *about* God—they may even know what He looks like; they can recognize His presence demonstrated in acts of miraculous intervention. But *recognizing* a person is different from actually *knowing* that person.

For example, I think I could recognize the President of the United States anywhere, but I do not have a face-to-face relationship with him. Therefore, I do not really *know* the President, even though I know a lot about him and could recognize him anywhere.

Moreover, if I were to call the White House to invite the President to a private lunch, I would not get very far. He would not know me from Adam because we have never had a face-to-face encounter. I have no access to the President because I do not have a *yada* relationship with him.

There is a difference between encountering God's goodness (as expressed in physical healing, forgiveness, intervention, provision, or blessing) and having a face-to-face encounter with God. If we desire to unlock Heaven, it is important to keep in mind that access and influence are granted through *yada*.

Jesus had continual, face-to-face encounters with His Father. Sure, He studied and even memorized the Scriptures, but His relationship was face-to-face. It was out of those personal encounters that Heaven was unlocked and the miraculous flowed naturally supernaturally.

Moses also had a face-to-face *yada* relationship with God. We see in Exodus 20:21 that the people Moses led, on the other hand, chose to distance themselves. Consequently, they were given the Law instead of relationship.

Religious performance is always the substitute for face-to-face encounters with God. But God's heart is to deliver us from the Law, and He offers personal relationship in its place. Jesus died on the cross simply to make a way for us to have a face-to-face relationship with the Father.

Sadly, some Christians view God as a benevolent absentee father who just sends the things we need and desire from afar. True, our heavenly Father does give us every good and perfect gift (see James 1:17), but He does so in the context of relationship. God desires to reveal Himself to His children every day in face-to-face encounters.

Part of the delight that I have in giving my children gifts is seeing their faces light up when they discover what I have hidden for them. I could not imagine the disappointment that I would feel if they took the gifts I had given them and went to their rooms to open them alone.

Our heavenly Father loves to give us the Kingdom, but He really wants to see our face as we open up Heaven to access what He has provided. Moreover, without the connection of personal relationship, gift-giving eventually loses its appeal for the giver and the recipient.

In Matthew 7:21-23, Jesus warned:

Not everyone who says to Me, "Lord, Lord," will enter the kingdom of heaven, but only he who does the will of My Father who is in heaven. Many will say to Me on that day, "Lord, Lord, did we not prophesy in Your name, and in Your name drive out demons and perform many miracles?" Then I will tell them plainly, "I never knew [ginosko/yada] you. Away from Me...."

God wants to have face-to-face encounters with us. He wants to know us, and He wants us to know Him. Signs and wonders, healing, miracles, and the prophetic are only authentic when they are born out of relationship in God's presence.

The apostle Paul, in Philippians 3:10, states, "I want to know [*yada/ginosko*] Christ and the power of His resurrection...." Notice that Paul desired to have a face-to-face encounter with Christ *before* he experienced the power of Christ.

Paul understood the priority of relationship in releasing the miraculous. Moreover, once we have an up-close, personal relationship with God, the supernatural becomes a natural outflow. Paul understood that the best way to live a naturally supernatural life is to encounter God face-to-face.

FRUITFULNESS FLOWS FROM INTIMACY

The fifth and final dimension of *yada* is sexual intimacy.[6] "Adam lay with [knew/*yada*] his wife Eve, and she became pregnant and gave birth to Cain..." (Gen. 4:1). In other words, Adam had sexual intercourse with Eve, and she became pregnant and had a son. Fruitfulness flows from intimacy. This principle is not only true in the natural, but also in the supernatural realm.

Just as Adam knew (*yada*) Eve and she became fruitful, bearing a son, so too, God desires us to be fruitful in bearing spiritual life. Fruitfulness, however, is born out of intimacy, which is rooted in knowing God in detail and with technical wisdom, which leads to a personal, face-to-face encounter.

Jesus operated in naturally supernatural ways because of His oneness and intimacy with His Father. Likewise, God desires to have comprehensive, *intimate* encounters with each one of us every day. In John 17:21-23, Jesus prayed:

That all of them [us] *may be one, Father, just as You are in Me and I am in You. May they also be in Us so that the world may believe that You have sent Me. I have given them the glory that You gave Me, that they may be one as We are one: I in them and You in Me....*

Certainly the Song of Solomon is a depiction of God's desire for intimacy with His people, His Bride. In the New Testament, we are described as the Bride of Christ (see Matt. 25:1-3; Rev. 19:7-8; 21:2-3), and Paul correlates the relationship of Christ and the Church to that of a husband and wife in marriage (see Eph. 5:22-33).

First John 3:9 points out that God's *seed* is in us, referring to the Holy Spirit residing inside of us. The Greek word for "seed" used in this passage is *sperma*, from which we get the English word *sperm*.[7] In other words, God has deposited His Holy Spirit inside of us through an intimate encounter, signifying an ongoing relationship of intimacy with us.

As we explored in the previous chapter, an authentic, supernatural lifestyle cannot be produced from religious formulas or techniques, but only through relationship with "our Father." It is only through intimacy with God that the miraculous is released in and through our lives.

HIDE AND SEEK

In Colossians 2:3, we are told, "In whom [Christ] are hidden all the treasures of wisdom and knowledge [*ginosko/yada*]." I love what my friend and colleague Bill Johnson says: "God hides things *for* us, not *from* us." God, in His infinite wisdom, designed His Kingdom so that we would have to look for truth. He created us to enjoy the adventure of discovery.

When my children were growing up, we would often play "hide and seek." There was an obvious thrill in their voices each time they pleaded with me to hide just one more time! There was exhilaration in their eyes as they anticipated the search and the surprise of finding me hidden out of sight in the closet or behind a door. "There you are! I found you!" they would excitedly exclaim each time.

Of course, there would be no enjoyment to the game if I simply stood behind them as they counted to ten with their eyes closed and if, when they opened them, they found me in the first two seconds of the search.

Conversely, if I hid myself so well that they could not find me, they would eventually give up and not want to play anymore. But because I wanted to be found, I would hide in such a way that they could find me once they had searched. Some people have stopped searching for God, thinking He has hidden from them and does not want to be found.

Our heavenly Father wants to be found. In Isaiah 55:6, we are encouraged to "seek the Lord while He may be found...." Jesus promised in Luke 11:9, "...Seek and you will find...." In James 4:8, we are reminded that if we come near to Him, He will come near to us. *Yada* means drawing near to God for an intimate encounter.

YADA IS THE ANSWER

In the first two chapters of the Book of Habakkuk, the prophet asks God for the solution to the world's problems. His complaint is basically that it seemed like the enemy was winning, like the wicked and wickedness were prevailing over the righteous and righteousness. And He asks God what He is going to do about it.

God's answer is found in Habakkuk 2:14: "The earth will be filled with the knowledge of the glory of the Lord, as the waters cover the sea."

For years, I quoted this verse as "The earth will be filled with the glory of the Lord," leaving out "the knowledge" (*yada*). There is a huge difference between the glory of the Lord simply covering the earth and our experience of the glory that is covering the earth. God wants us to personally experience His glory in our lives. He wants us to have a personal, detailed, intimate, face-to-face encounter with His glory.

Many believers are searching for the keys to unlock the power of the Kingdom of God. I used to imagine the glory of the Lord coming to earth in the form of a cloud that everyone could look up at and see with the natural eye. I soon realized, however, that the glory was intended to come through our lives. We are the answer to the problems in the world today. The glory of God is seen when people are healed, saved, and delivered (which is the full definition of the Greek word commonly translated "salvation": *sozo*[8]).

God wants to use us to change the world. We are the answer—the solution for the world; it is "Christ in you the hope of glory" (Col. 1:27). But, before God's glory can flow *through* us, we must experience His glory, His presence, *in* us.

The supernatural lifestyle flows out of a *yada* relationship with God. In John 15:5, Jesus said, "...If a man remains in Me and I in him, he will bear much fruit; apart from Me you can do nothing." The more we live in a *yada* relationship with God, remaining in Him, the more we will see His Kingdom coming to earth and manifestations of His glory for all to encounter.

On the first night of a Firestorm conference in Yuma, Arizona, a woman came who had fourth-stage breast cancer. She was scheduled for surgery the next day, so when her friend invited her to the meeting, the woman agreed, even though she was a Jehovah's Witness.

During the meeting, the woman received prayer, and had an encounter with God's presence. She felt the power of God engulfing her entire body; His love seemed to consume every cell. She obviously had never experienced anything like this before. After a few minutes of encountering God's glory, she exclaimed that all of the lumps in her breasts had disappeared, and the pain was completely gone!

The next day, the woman went to the hospital for her scheduled surgery. Perplexed, she began to share with the staff about how the lumps in her breasts had disappeared and the pain had completely left the night before. After a thorough examination, the medical team reported that there was no sign of cancer and cancelled the surgery.

The woman raced back home, called her friend, and accepted Jesus into her life on the spot. That night she brought to the meeting several other family members, who also gave their hearts to the Lord. Most likely, no amount of arguing would have won that woman and her family to Christ, but one encounter with God's love, demonstrated through the healing of her body, convinced her.

Signs and wonders are needed to convince the world, but the object must always be to introduce them to a growing, personal, intimate, face-to-face, daily encounter with God. We can only give out of what we have received in His presence. So, I want to encourage you: *yada, yada, yada*. The world is waiting for God's glory to cover the earth through you, one encounter at a time!

ENDNOTES

1. Gerhard Kittle, *Theological Dictionary of the New Testament,* vol. 1 (Grand Rapids, MI: Eerdmans, 1964), 689-714; Colin Brown, *The New International Dictionary of New Testament*

Theology, vol. 2 (Grand Rapids, MI: Zondervan, 1967), 392-409.

2. Ibid.

3. Ibid.

4. Ibid.

5. Ibid.

6. Ibid.

7. James Strong, "Greek Dictionary," *The New Strong's Expanded Exhaustive Concordance of the Bible* (Nashville, TN: Thomas Nelson, 2001), "sperma" (#4690).

8. *The New Testament Greek Lexicon,* s.v. "sozo," http://www.studylight.org/lex/grk/view.cgi?number=4982 (accessed Nov. 15, 2008).

Chapter 4

REVIVAL REST

WHILE driving down the freeway one day, my eyes were drawn toward a billboard advertising a deserted, white Jamaican beach lined with beautiful, green palm trees and crystal blue water. The caption read, "Want to get away?" Immediately, I felt like calling the travel agent and making arrangements to book a flight that very afternoon!

Wouldn't it be great if we could just take a vacation on the spur of the moment whenever we wanted one? Some of us might not work again, especially if we could get *paid* vacations whenever we wanted! Even the thought of getting a break from the busyness of life can provide some measure of relief.

On the other hand, I am amazed at how I can take a two-week vacation and then still feel like I need a two-week vacation when I get back! I pack so many exciting activities into those two weeks that I usually do not have any time to rest.

Similarly, as Christians, we can get caught up in religious performance and striving for God's acceptance, only to be left with an insatiable need for more. Striving in our own strength to release the Kingdom of God in signs and wonders, miracles, healing, and the prophetic can lead to performance anxiety, resulting in spiritual, emotional, and physical exhaustion.

I have come to learn that, while relaxing on a beach in Jamaica is a wonderful diversion, true rest comes from within, not from our external environment. Working and striving in the Kingdom may give us temporary fulfillment, but rest that lasts comes from acceptance and approval in what Jesus has already provided for us.

In Matthew 11:28-30, Jesus gave this invitation:

Come to Me, all you who are weary and burdened, and I will give you rest. Take My yoke upon you and learn from Me, for I am gentle and humble in heart, and you will find rest for your souls. For My yoke is easy and My burden is light.

In this passage, Jesus speaks to those who are exhausted in their religious efforts to experience true spiritual life. He provides an escape for those who are burdened by religious striving and performance (trying to gain God's acceptance and approval). Like the invitation on the freeway billboard, Jesus offers a permanent spiritual vacation—a get-away from religious works.

The context for this invitation occurs in Matthew 11:20-24, in which Jesus describes the miracles that took place in the various cities He had visited. Despite these miracles, however, the religious leaders rejected the revelation of truth; they refused to repent and come to Jesus. Instead, they were content to rely upon religious performance and good works to gain God's approval.

Jesus implies that they will never find true rest, despite all of their religious efforts. In fact, they will actually heap judgment on themselves if they continue to reject the truth found in Him. Jesus is the only place to find true spiritual rest. Thus, the harder the religious try, the less effective they are in their spirituality.

On the other hand, little children are able to see their need for Jesus. Only those who recognize their inability to perform have the wherewithal to enter into spiritual rest. Of course, rest is an invitation extended to everyone, but only those who humble themselves like a child will be able to access it.

A similar argument is made in the Book of Hebrews, written to Hebrew Christians who were being tempted to turn back to Judaism to escape persecution. They were of the notion that God would still accept them, without appropriating the sacrifice of Christ, as long as they fulfilled the religious requirements of the Law.

The point is made throughout the book, however, that only those who *continue* to live in Jesus by faith are able to live in the spiritual rest that God has promised (see Heb. 2:1-4; 3:1;12-14; 4:1; 6:1-12; 10:19-23;32-36; 12:1-3,25—actually, just read the whole Book of Hebrews).

Specifically, in chapter 3, the correlation is made between the Promised Land that the children of Israel entered into after their deliverance from slavery in Egypt and the spiritual Sabbath rest that Jesus offers. In chapter 4, rest is equated with the continuous Sabbath rest that God took in Genesis 2. The only way to enter into this rest, however, is through faith in Christ and His sacrificial work on the cross.

Revival rest means operating out of acceptance and approval in Christ, based upon the work that He completed on the cross. Revival rest means relaxing in God's presence, where there is no need for performance. It is only in this place of spiritual rest that our need for striving and performance ceases to consume our energies.

JUST RELAX

I lived in Huntington Beach, California, for several years, where I loved to body board. I especially loved the thrill of catching a double-overhead wave that had the potential of pounding the life out me. I know that sounds demented, but there is no reward without risk—the higher the danger, the greater the rush!

When I was first learning how to ride waves, I went out on a small, four-foot day. I was having a lot of fun being thrown over the "falls" and crashing around in the churning whitewater. The water was only about shoulder high, so there seemed to be no imminent danger of drowning.

Then, without any warning, a rogue set of waves came rolling in that looked like mountainous cliffs as they rapidly approached. My first instinct was to run, but since I was in water, I began to swim toward the shore. The current, however, began to pull me out toward the oncoming gargantuan waves, and immediately, I realized that it was useless to try to escape.

I turned around toward the ocean, and I began to paddle for all I was worth in an attempt to get over the first wave, measuring about 10 feet high. (When you are on your stomach, 10 feet looks like 20!) I got about halfway up the face of the wave when I realized that I was not going to make it.

The powerful wave pitched me backward, causing me to land upside down in the water. Immediately, I was in "the spin cycle" and did not know which way was up. Furthermore, the impact of hitting the water with such force took most of my breath away. I could feel every muscle in my body tense up in response to the panic that I was experiencing.

The wave was relentless. Just as I would almost make it to the surface, the power of the wave would suck me back into the depths. It seemed like some invisible force was bound and determined to make me "submit" as it held me under the water. Full of terror, I continued to struggle with every ounce of energy I could muster.

Breathless, I finally struggled to the surface, coughing up salt water and gasping for air. As I looked up, I could not believe my eyes; another wave, a little larger than the first, was coming fast upon me. I was now trapped in the impact zone, and before I could get a full breath of air, the next mountain crashed onto me, sending me somersaulting to the bottom of the ocean that was now about ten feet deep.

Once again, I struggled, feeling like a rag doll being shaken underneath the water. Once again, I came up gasping for air and coughing up the sea that had filled my lungs.

Once again, another wave, larger than the last, pummeled me without mercy. This time, I could feel the air being pulled out of every blood cell in my body, and I knew that I was going to die.

In that moment, I remembered someone telling me that the best way to get back to the surface was by relaxing. Under the water, however, it seemed so unnatural to just rest while I was in such a perilous situation.

Since I no longer had enough strength to fight my way to the surface, I decided to relax and accept the consequences. I also prayed, "God, if You get me out of this predicament...."

Oddly enough, as soon as I relaxed, I could feel myself rising toward the surface, and I popped up, took two or three big breaths, and the "set wave" came crashing down on me, throwing me into the spin cycle one more time.

This time, instead of struggling for the surface, I simply rested, knowing that the air inside of my lungs would float me to freedom. Sure enough, in just a few seconds I was at the surface, but thoroughly exhausted from my near-death experience. I finally made it back to shore, where I looked like a beached whale lying on the sand, still coughing up salt water.

I have been in similar waves since, and while they are still intimidating, I have learned to relax, even though I am sometimes tempted to fight my way through them. I have come to realize that my best effort is no match for the power of the sea.

I often feel the same way when someone approaches me with an overwhelming physical disability that needs to be healed. In my desire to facilitate their seemingly impossible miracle breakthrough, I am often tempted to work harder for what has already been provided through Christ's sacrificial work on the cross. During those times, when I feel the need to perform, I have to remind myself to relax and let God's supernatural Kingdom power work through me naturally.

A TESTIMONY FOR SUNDAY

Whenever I speak somewhere, I try to bring some students from our School of Supernatural Ministry. I love to activate them whenever I have the opportunity during the various meetings. Often I will invite them on the stage to give prophetic words, as well as words of knowledge pertaining to physical ailments that are represented in the audience.

On one occasion, I was assigning specific time slots for various students to share testimonies of how God had used them to heal people in and outside of the church. I came to Joe, and he turned white with fear when I informed him that he, too, was going to give a testimony. He sheepishly explained that, while he had been in the school for a year, he had never actually prayed for someone who had been healed, although he had seen others do it.

I told him not to worry: "By Sunday morning, you will have a testimony." I also informed him that he would be sharing on Sunday morning. His face turned five shades whiter. I encouraged him to relax and just release what was already inside of him, and I told him that he would participate in someone's healing before Sunday morning.

On Saturday night, I invited all of the students to the stage to give words of knowledge, and then I had them go out to the audience to pray for those with the ailments they had identified. Joe had the impression that God wanted to heal someone's knee. About 20 minutes into the prayer time, Joe started jumping up and down, along with the person he had been praying for. "He's healed! He's healed!" Joe shouted over and over.

I brought them to the stage, where the man shared how he had severed his ACL ligament 16 years prior and could not bend his knee, let alone put weight on it while bending it. On cue, he began doing deep knee bends, he jumped up and down, and then he proceeded to run and dance around the auditorium, demonstrating his repaired ligament. The crowd went wild because they all knew him quite well and were aware of his previous debilitation.

On Sunday morning, Joe shared with the congregation how he had felt besieged with anxiety at the thought of giving a testimony about healing when he had not seen anyone healed. He went on to share that, as he began to interview the man with the "knee problem," he was completely exasperated when he discovered that the man not only needed a miracle, but a creative miracle at that!

He told of how he had utilized every principle he had ever been taught related to healing, but that nothing had worked. Finally, out of utter frustration, he said, "I'm just going to do what Kevin does: I'm just going to relax and release the Father's presence."

He then broke into a huge smile and announced that, as soon as he had stopped striving and had simply rested in God's presence, a fire came on the man's leg, and he was instantly healed! Joe is no longer intimidated by praying for the sick because he has discovered the Kingdom key of revival rest.

Swing Easy

Revival rest is like a well-timed golf swing. When I approach the first tee, I routinely remind myself to relax and swing nice and easy. I have found that, the easier I swing, the farther and straighter the ball travels. Having that knowledge in mind during my pre-swing routine usually helps me to swing nice and easy, releasing a crushing 275-yard drive straight down the middle of the fairway.

When I get to the second tee, however, I am usually feeling very powerful, thinking I could smash a 300-yard drive if I just gave a little more effort. The result is often a snap hook, slice, or a grounder that barely makes it to the women's tee box.

Embarrassed at the result, I proceed to use my "mulligan," and regroup. In my mind, I rehearse hitting the next tee shot about 150 yards. Amazingly, after accentuating a slow, easy swing, sometimes the ball *will* travel as far as 300 yards (of course, that's when hitting it downhill with a tailwind)!

Similarly, I have learned that I get a lot more distance in releasing the supernatural resources of the Kingdom when I relax in revival rest. The more I strive in trying to release the Kingdom, the less effective my efforts become. I am learning more and more to trust that less is more when it comes to unlocking Heaven and living a naturally supernatural life.

A few years ago, my wife suffered from a rare outbreak of hives. After several months of experimenting with various prescriptions, the dermatologists finally informed her that there were no more alternatives—there was no cure. She was in constant discomfort, especially during the sleep hours when the pressure of the covers and lying on the bed would cause a breakout of the hives. Her only comfort was to take a hot bath a few times during the night. Needless to say, she did not get a lot of rest during that ordeal.

We had been praying every prayer we could think of, and even fasting, in our attempts to get breakthrough healing. We went to several people who had "the gift" of healing, but still there was no change in her condition. After several months of disappointment after disappointment, we were emotionally exhausted in our efforts.

Finally, one morning my wife announced that she was completely healed. She explained that, during the night, I had put my hand on her stomach. Immediately, she felt a fire go through her body. All of the itching ceased, and she was able to sleep through the rest of the night with no irritation to her skin. The amazing thing was that I did not remember putting my hand on her stomach. I was sound asleep!

That is the epitome of swinging easy. There was obviously no effort involved at all on my part; I just swung my arm over. When it comes to releasing the Kingdom to those around us who need supernatural intervention, we would do well to remember that less is more as it relates to our efforts to perform.

Jesus Worked So That We Don't Have To

In Genesis 1, we find a description of what took place during the six days of creation. After each day's work, we are told that there was a night and a day, and then the next day's work would begin. Each day's work had a beginning and an end—a specific time frame.

Finally, on the seventh day, after God had finished all of the work of creation, He rested. Interestingly, there is no mention of a night and day (see Gen. 2:2-3), the implication being that God continued to rest once He had completed the work He had intended. Moreover, nowhere in Scripture are we told that God went back to tinker with creation once He entered into rest. Once He was done, He was done.

On the cross, Jesus declared, in John 19:30, "It is finished." What was finished? Jesus fulfilled all of the work required in purchasing our salvation. He accomplished everything that the Father had given Him to do in order to restore our rightful inheritance in the Kingdom.

More importantly, He worked so that we could rest. He provided a way for us to take a permanent spiritual vacation from all religious striving and performance in our attempts to please God and man. When Jesus announced that it was finished, He meant it—it's over. No more work is required or desired.

In Second Corinthians 5:17, we are told, "If anyone is in Christ, he is a new creation; the old has gone, the new has come!" So then, just as God rested after creating in Genesis 1, we are invited into spiritual rest as a result of God's making us new in Christ. No more work is required; no additions are necessary; we are simply invited to rest as the new creation Jesus has made us to be.

The Labor Day holiday in America came out of the Industrial Revolution of the 1800s. It was common practice in those times for employees to be required to work seven days a week, 12 hours per day, with no breaks and only a short lunch. No vacations, holidays, sick days, or personal days were allowed. Fortunately, it was not long before that changed. Workers banded together to form unions to fight for, and protect, the human rights of the employed.

After many battles with industrialists, on September 5, 1882, all of the unions combined forces, and 10,000 industry workers marched together in a parade to protest for better working conditions. After the parade, despite the danger of meeting publicly to defy the industrialists, they joined together for a picnic to celebrate their efforts.

Although there were many future battles fought for labor rights, the unions were able to establish the work week that many of us enjoy today, in which we are expected to work for eight hours, to recreate for eight hours, and to rest for eight hours. We are able to take scheduled breaks, lunch breaks, vacations, sick days, and even personal days because of what others accomplished on our behalf.[1]

It is the same way in the Kingdom. Jesus created a new labor pact through which we are permitted to rest.

RESTING WHILE WE WORK

At this point, some may be asking about the Scriptures that speak of working. For example, Jesus declared that He and His Father are always working (see John 5:17).

There is no account of Jesus ever taking a vacation. He is still working today. When you pray, you will never get a recorded message saying: "God is on vacation and will not be able to work a miracle until He gets back in two weeks. Until then, just hang in there and work it out yourself." On the other hand, Jesus was always resting. He did not need a vacation because He was continually working from a place of rest.

True, God is always working, but He is not striving in Heaven trying to release His Kingdom, nor is He performing for us in an attempt to gain our approval. Whatever supernatural intervention comes to us is a natural over-flow of who He is—His nature. God is not in Heaven striving to produce results. No, He continually works from a place of rest in order to bring His Kingdom to earth.

In Matthew 9:37-38, Jesus looks for those who will work in the harvest fields. The apostle Paul encourages us to respect all of those who work hard (see 1 Thess. 5:12) and exhorts: "Whatever you do, work at it with all your heart..." (Col. 3:23). In fact, if we do not work, the Kingdom will not be released to those around us. Like God, however, we are called to work from the place of revival rest in order to bring His Kingdom to earth. As we learn to work in rest, we will begin to be effective in living a naturally supernatural life.

When I was in Bible college, I worked part-time at United Parcel Service. It was the most physically demanding work I have ever done, even though it was only four hours a day.

I started out as a "flipper." My job was to "flip" the boxes label-up and position them in single file as they came down the conveyor belt in a massive heap. Then the "pullers" could take the appropriate package for their truck as they passed by.

As the boxes came toward me *en masse*, I would have to hold them off with my shoulder while I arranged what I could. It would not be long until there was a mound of boxes piled on the floor next to me, as well as on the bottom return belt, that I had been unable to flip and that were missed by the "pullers."

After the first week, I had bruises from head to toe and had lost several pounds in sweat. I found out later that most people quit at the first break! I felt like quitting every day at the first break. For the first month, I came home beat up and exhausted every night. Every muscle in my body ached. I even dreamt of parcels attacking me in the middle of the night.

One day, shortly after that first month, everything just seemed to click. I could flip the boxes with one hand, lining them up in single file, while carrying on a conversation. Soon I was laughing throughout the shift and felt completely energized afterward. The job became easy, and I was soon promoted several times because of the effectiveness of my work. In fact, the more I rested while I worked, the more productive I became.

WHO WANTS ARTIFICIAL FRUIT?

In John 15:5, Jesus states: "I am the vine; you are the branches. If a man remains in Me and I in him, he will bear much fruit; apart from Me you can do nothing." Fruitfulness flows out of rest. In this passage, Jesus is speaking of revival rest. It is only those who remain (rest) in Him who will bear Kingdom fruit.

I believe that Jesus was not only referring to the consistency of remaining in Him, but also to the quality in which someone remains in Him. Remaining in Him has to do with resting in Him—resting in the work that He has provided for us, as well as resting in His presence.

Developing the character of Christ and releasing the Kingdom of Christ should be a natural outgrowth of the rest that we experience as we remain in Him. It is as we rest in His presence, soaking in the nutrients of His love and grace, that we are able to produce Kingdom fruit.

Think about it: what does an apple seed do to produce fruit? Does it strive and struggle to produce a trunk, as if it will not develop without effort? Does the trunk grimace as it pushes out the limbs to provide a place for fruitfulness to grow? Do the limbs muster up every ounce of performance to produce the fruit?

When we strive to produce Kingdom fruit in the effort of our own performance, artificial fruit is the result. Who likes artificial fruit? Who would buy artificial fruit, even if it were half-priced? Have you ever bitten into an artificial apple? Once, as a kid, I bit into an artificial apple and got a mouthful of wax. I never did that again.

Artificial fruit is like religion. In Genesis 1:28, God told Adam to be *fruitful* and increase, not to *strive* and increase. Once again, authentic fruitfulness in the Kingdom of God comes from rest.

God always intended for man to live in revival rest. In the Garden of Eden, man was supposed to continually eat of the tree of life (a symbol of Jesus, the vine, in John 15), which denoted the presence of God. It was in this place of fellowship and communion that Adam and Eve enjoyed supernatural rest and fruitfulness.

When Adam and Eve decided to eat of the tree of the knowledge of good and evil, however, their effort to be like God and attempt to attain wisdom apart from God led to religious performance, which produced artificial fruit, resulting in death.

Conversely, when we live in revival rest, we become naturally fruitful. When we eat of the tree of life, Jesus, the True Vine, provides the supernatural nutrients to produce supernatural breakthrough. The surest way to release the Kingdom, to be fruitful, is through revival rest.

DRIVE-BY HEALINGS

Peter is a great example of someone who operated in the supernatural out of rest. Acts 5:15 implies that people were healed as Peter's shadow fell on them. He was not even trying to heal people! He was just continually resting in God's presence, being a habitation of His presence, and then, effortlessly leaking what was inside of him. That is the natural outflow of revival rest. As we remain in the presence of Jesus, supernatural Kingdom fruit will result.

My son, Chad, was part of a small ministry team that our church sent to the Houston Astrodome right after the devastation of Hurricane Katrina. They were able to pray for many people who desperately needed physical healing.

On one occasion, Chad was praying for a woman on a cot. As he was releasing God's presence to her, a man who was walking by shouted out, "What the —— did you just do to me?" Chad looked up toward the startled man and assured him that he had not done anything. The man shot back, "Yes, you did! As I was walking past you, my knee felt like it was on fire! What did you do?" Chad explained that he was just praying for the woman on the cot.

After further inquiry, the man explained that he had had a knee injury that had debilitated him for years. As he was limping past Chad, the fire hit his knee, and he was completely healed. Chad explained that the power of God must have leaked onto the man as Chad was praying for the woman. The man received Jesus on the spot and left very happy!

I have had several occasions when I just put my hand on someone's shoulder, arm, or back while saying hello, only to find out that, as I touched them, they were completely healed. I call these "drive-by healings." They happen apart from any personal effort to release God's Kingdom; they are simply a result of living in revival rest.

When we live in revival rest, fruitfulness is a natural byproduct. The Kingdom that is expanding within us, like the apple seed in the soil, will naturally begin to manifest in the external environment around us.

A classic example of this dynamic happened when Jesus was sleeping (resting) in the middle of a storm (see Mark 4:35-41). Overwhelmed by the circumstances, the disciples woke Jesus to inform Him that they were all about to die. Jesus spoke to the storm out of the rest that He was living in, and immediately, the internal environment in Jesus transformed the external environment around Him, causing the storm to cease.

Kingdom fruitfulness comes from revival rest. The more we cultivate our relationship with the true vine, the tree of life, and rest in His presence, the more we will naturally find ourselves releasing the Kingdom to those around us. I want to encourage you to pursue a naturally supernatural life while operating out of revival rest.

ENDNOTE

1. "Labor Day History," http://www.history.com/content/laborday/labor-history (accessed Dec. 30, 2008).

Chapter 5

THE SUPERNATURAL POWER OF OVERFLOWING JOY

I was in Miami, Florida, speaking at a conference on healing, when a woman came into the meeting aided by a walker and assisted by two ushers and her husband, who helped her take a seat in the back of the auditorium. I especially noticed her because it took them about five minutes to get her situated.

After the message, the two ushers approached me and asked if I would go to the woman and pray for her. I expressed that I would be happy to pray for her, but I said that she should come up to the front if she wanted to be healed. Sometimes faith needs an activity.

I went on to pray for a few more people, and after about ten minutes, I noticed the woman standing at the front of the auditorium, leaning on her walker. As I approached her, I noticed that she seemed to be in her late 50s and was obviously very weak. She was barely able to stand, even with the aid of her walker in front and her husband behind, propping her up.

As I began to interview her, I found out that she was only 40 years old. She had been in kidney failure for quite some time and had been bed-ridden for three months, which had sucked the life out of her. Her husband and two teenage daughters had become her round-the-clock aids, leaving her feeling like a burden.

When I asked what she wanted, her face became even more distraught as she replied: "I want to be healed, but I don't think I can be."

"Why not?" I countered.

"Well," she said, "I felt so guilty over not being able to care for my family due to my illness that I finally went down to the transplant center and put my name on the list for a kidney transplant."

She went on to say that her relatives, who were leaders at another church, had told her that, by putting her name on the list, she had disqualified herself for a miracle by her lack of faith. They told her that God would never listen to her prayer for healing because she had trusted in medical treatment over miraculous intervention.

Without hesitation, I responded: "No way! Your faith is standing right here, right now. In fact, I see the Father smiling over you right now; He is so pleased with you. No. More than that—He's dancing around you as He's smiling. Even more than that, He's smiling, He's dancing, and I see Him laughing over you. He is so happy with you!"

At that, I put my hand on her head and began to laugh in response to the scene that I had just envisioned. She began to laugh as well, and together we continued laughing hysterically for about three minutes.

Suddenly, she looked at me with widened eyes and yelled out, "I'm on fire! I'm on fire! Fan me off! Fan me off!" as she placed her hand on her kidney. Hearing the alarm in her voice, her husband began furiously waving his hands over her kidney, fanning it off.

We continued laughing for a few more minutes until she yelled out once again, "It's in my feet! It's in my feet! Fan me off!" On cue, her husband got on his knees and began fanning her feet with his hands as the woman and I continued to laugh uncontrollably and to sway and contort with joy, my hand still locked onto her hair.

Then, without any advance notice, she backed away from her walker, bent down, and jumped into mid-air, doing a make-shift karate kick. She did this, despite the fact that previously she could not even get into a chair on her own, let alone jump into the air like Michael Jordan!

She began running around me, laughing and shouting, "I'm healed! I'm healed!" After circling a few times, she hurled herself into a chair on the front row and leaped out of it as though she had been shot from a cannon. Everything in her countenance and body language seemed to come to life. She looked 20 years younger; the transformation was stunning.

There happened to be a kidney specialist at the meeting who examined her on the spot and declared that she had no visible symptoms of kidney failure. The next Monday, when she went into the transplant office, the doctor was baffled because she had somehow already received a brand-new kidney!

God gave her a brand-new kidney as we simply laughed. There were no drawn-out prayers or pleading—just laughter. That is the supernatural power of overflowing joy.

In Proverbs 17:22, Solomon points out that, "A cheerful heart is good medicine...." The New American Standard Bible says, "A joyful heart...." Over the years, I have found that the joy of the Lord, the medicine from Heaven, has been very effective in releasing the supernatural power of God. It was certainly the case for this woman who needed a new kidney. Until she received the medicine from Heaven—joy—her only alternative for health was a medical transplant.

Joy Is Normal

One third of the Kingdom of God is joy. In Romans 14:17, we are told, "The kingdom of God is not a matter of eating and drinking, but of righteousness, peace, and joy in the Holy Spirit." In Psalm 16:11, we learn, "...In Your presence is fullness of joy, at Your right hand are pleasures forevermore" (NKJV). Joy is one of the primary characteristics of the Kingdom of God because joy is one of the primary characteristics of the King.

So then, when the Kingdom comes, joy is expected. It is normal to experience joy in God's presence. Even the angels rejoice when one sinner repents (see Luke 15:10), which implies that there is a constant party of joy in Heaven because people on earth are constantly coming into right relationship with God.

Jesus taught His disciples to pray, "...On earth as it is in heaven" (Matt. 6:10). So then, if there is joy in Heaven, it only makes sense that there should be joy on the earth as well. Joy should be the normal lifestyle for the Christian.

Joy is one of the fruits of the Spirit (see Gal. 5:22). Therefore, joy should be a natural outgrowth of living in the Spirit—God's presence. In First Thessalonians 5:16, we are commanded, "Be joyful always." In other words, joy should be cultivated as a daily lifestyle; it should be a continual occurrence, not just a once-in-a-while event.

The apostle Paul wrote from prison and encouraged the Christians at Philippi with these words: "Rejoice in the Lord always. [And, just in case you did not get it the first time] I will say it again: Rejoice" (Phil. 4:4). In other words, keep doing joy over and over again.

Joy should be expected by the righteous. In the Book of Job, Bildad attempted to comfort Job with this promise: "Surely God does not reject a blameless man or strengthen the hands of the evildoers. He will yet fill your mouth with laughter and your lips with shouts of joy" (Job 8:20-21). God's intention for us is joy and laughter.

When the Galatian Christians, influenced by false teachers, were considering returning to the Law of Judaism in order to escape the persecution that came from their identification with Christ, Paul's response was: "What has happened to all your joy..." (Gal. 4:15). He was basically saying, if following the Law is so great, if living under religious restrictions is so freeing, then why are you so sad? Where is the joy?—because the evidence of being in right relationship with God is joy.

When David repented over his sin with Bathsheba, he was only concerned with two things. First, he prayed that God would not cast him from His presence or take the Holy Spirit from him, and second, he prayed that the joy of salvation would be restored (see Ps. 51:11-12).

As believers, it is normal for us to experience joy in the Kingdom of God; it is normal for us to desire the joy of Heaven on earth. Furthermore, whenever the Kingdom (His presence) comes, joy should be the result.

Isaiah prophesied that the Messiah, the Christ, would bring the oil of gladness (see Isa. 61:3) and everlasting joy (see Isa. 61:7). When the angel of the Lord announced the birth of Jesus, he said, "...I bring you good news of great joy that will be for all the people" (Luke 2:10).

Even before Jesus was born, Mary went to visit her cousin Elizabeth, and as soon as John, in Elizabeth's womb, encountered Jesus, in Mary's womb, he leaped for joy (see Luke 1:41). When Jesus shows up, joy will be the normal response.

The Church should be the happiest place on planet Earth. The Church should be the place where people can truly find "Happy Hour." A fast-food restaurant should not be the only place that offers a "Happy Meal." The

Church should be the place where people can laugh in the freedom of God's presence. The Church should be an attraction of joy.

JOY = HAPPINESS

In Matthew 5:1-12, Jesus teaches the disciples what we have now come to know as "The Beatitudes." There are several of them, and each one begins with the Greek adjective, *makarios* (the verb form is makarizo in Luke 1:48, and the noun form is makarismos in Galatians 4:15).[1] This word is translated as "blessed" in the New International Version.

Unfortunately, the translating committee did not do justice to the meaning of the Greek word, *makarios*. The Greek word, *makarios* (*makarizo/makarismos*), comes from two words. The first is *mak,* which means "huge," and from which we get the English word *macro*—huge (like the McDonald's Big Mac). The second word is *rizo,* which means "happy." *Makarizo,* then, means "hugely happy."

In Matthew 5:6, for example, Jesus really said, "*Hugely happy* are those who hunger and thirst for righteousness, for they will be filled." Filled with what? They will be filled with God's presence, and in His presence is the fullness of joy (hugely happy)!

The word *makarios* (*makarizo/makarismos*) originated in the Alexandrian classical Greek times, and has the connotation of being so happy that circumstances—anything in this life—or death cannot touch it.[2] It is so huge that nothing can withstand its power. It is what Jesus promised to those who would come to Him.

I used to think that joy was different from happiness. I had always been taught that happiness was rooted in a "happening" and, therefore, was circumstantial, whereas joy was an internal continual state of being with no connection to external conditions. Happiness was expressed by external manifestations while joy was defined by the quiet confidence that everything would work out for good in the future.

Upon reflection, I realized that I really used to define joy as "peace." Joy was the ability to "hang in there" until Jesus came back to deliver me from life's problems and challenges. I used to always quote the verse, "...Who for the joy set before Him endured the cross..." (Heb. 12:2), proving that Jesus put off happiness in this life (enduring the cross) for something more substantial (joy) when He got to Heaven. But my understanding of joy and happiness changed when I started to learn about *makarios*.

OUR ORDER IS NOT NECESSARILY GOD'S ORDER

You might be thinking at this point that laughter in the Church can be out of order. True, but so can singing, prophecy, tongues, dancing, and on and on. We are not to discontinue these things just because there is a possibility of disorder. We are to pastor them.

I would caution, however, that our sense of order might be a lot different from God's sense of order. We tend to think of order as everything being in nice, neat rows, at 90-degree angles, and perfectly level. God's sense of order is mountains popping up all over the place and winding rivers and trees strewn every which way with no semblance of purpose. A pine tree grows next to a fir tree at a different height.

In creation, almost nothing is level; there are few 90-degree angles, and nice, neat rows are a rarity. Those things are all man's sense of order. God's sense of order can look pretty messy and disorderly from our perspective.

In Second Samuel 6, when the Ark of the Covenant (the presence of God) was returned to Israel, David got pretty wild and crazy in his celebration. His wife, Michal, looked on the scene with disdain, believing he was out of order in his exuberant behavior.

David's response is insightful: "It was before the Lord...I will celebrate before the Lord. I will become even more undignified than this, and I will be humiliated in my own eyes..." (2 Sam. 6:21-22).

As for Michal, she became barren (unfruitful) as a result of her open display of disgust. She failed to recognize that it is appropriate to be wild in celebration of God's presence, and she mocked that which was valued by God.

Some are afraid that the flesh will get out of control when there is too much laughter. Some even refer to appropriate laughter as "holy laughter," as though they want to distinguish between laughing in the "Spirit" and laughing in the "flesh" (human origin).

In Psalm 84:2, David says, "My soul longed and even yearned for the courts of the Lord; my heart and *my flesh* sing for joy to the living God" (NASB). When our laughter is generated by God, even our natural flesh (our humanity) is involved. It is appropriate to have joy and to laugh in God's house as He reveals His greatness.

I used to have access to front-row seats at the old Forum, where the Los Angeles Lakers used to play back in the 1980s, affectionately known by fans as the "Showtime" era. I had the privilege of being at the Forum on the night in 1988 when they won the NBA title against the "Bad Boys" of Detroit—the Pistons.

When Kareem, Magic, Worthy, Rambis (Rambo), Scott, Cooper (Coop), A.C. Green, and others won the decisive game seven, the Forum erupted in celebration. Grown men, sophisticated businessmen, were jumping off of chairs in celebration of the victory. They rushed the floor, shouting, screaming, giving high-fives, and throwing beer on each other without shame. They were out of control.

Their emotions were appropriate, however, because the environment promoted such behavior. In fact, if they had just sat in their seats in that environment, offering a golf-clap, they would have been accused of being Pistons' fans. When in the Forum on a history-making night, it is considered normal to express extreme exuberance.

How much more so in the house of God! In Psalm 20:5, David describes the environment this way: "We will shout for joy when You are victorious...." In Psalm 105:43, David observes: "He brought out His people with rejoicing, His chosen ones with shouts of joy." It is normal to express extreme exuberance in God's presence.

Unfortunately, joy is *not* a normal lifestyle for many Christians. We are taught in church that laughter is inappropriate and that crying is a sign that the Spirit is moving. Uncontrolled laughter is viewed as immature and out of order in a church service, but if someone cries throughout a message, we consider it a normal response.

As children, most of us were told to stop laughing in public settings and to act like adults. We learned from an early age that mature people do not laugh uncontrollably; but crying uncontrollably is acceptable, especially in church.

We were taught to control ourselves, that we should only laugh in church in response to a good joke that is told by the pastor from the pulpit. There is something inherently wrong when we limit the joy of the Lord to a well-timed joke.

Additionally, there is an underlying mindset that Christians are not to live by feelings, but by faith. True, feelings should not affect my faith, but faith should affect my feelings. If my faith is in the God of the impossible, then I can live in joy and happiness in any circumstance. Even if I do not feel joy, I can choose to laugh through any hardship by faith, based on the truth that God is always good, despite my circumstances.

Laughter is a choice. If through self-control we can stop laughing, then we can choose to start laughing whenever we want. Self-control—as a fruit of the Spirit (see Gal. 5:23)—is characterized by choosing to do the good, not just abstaining from the bad. Furthermore, like any other fruit of the Spirit, self-control and joy are to be cultivated; we are to grow so that these characteristics are continuously more evident in our daily lives.

Joy is not an inherent human characteristic. It is something that must be cultivated through the Holy Spirit. Even Jesus cultivated joy as He accessed Heaven through the Holy Spirit. Luke tells us that Jesus was "full of joy through the Holy Spirit" (Luke 10:21).

Therefore, fullness of joy and *makarios* are always possible when we live in the realm of Heaven, in His presence, through the Holy Spirit. In His presence, in Heaven, is fullness of joy.

JOY COMES IN THE *MOURNING*

Certainly, crying, sorrow, and mourning are a part of life, but it is not God's goal for us to remain there. Solomon observes: "There is a time for everything...a time to weep and a time to laugh..." (Eccles. 3:1,4). Moreover, we are encouraged to mourn with those who mourn (see Rom. 12:15).

An important aspect of the Messianic call in Isaiah 61 was to comfort all who mourn (see Isa. 61:2). Jesus demonstrated this best when He wept over His best friend, Lazarus, who had died (see John 11:35). In Second Corinthians 1:3, God is described as "the Father of compassion and the God of all comfort."

Crying, however, is not meant to last. It is not normal for a believer to spend his or her whole life in sadness. In Psalm 30:5, David provides hope with these words: "...Weeping may remain for a night, but rejoicing [joy] comes in the morning."

A pastor friend of mine used to always greet me with, "Good morning," regardless of the time. One day I asked him why he would use that greeting in the evening. His response was astounding: "Kevin, it is always morning in the Kingdom, and joy comes in the morning." From God's perspective, it is always a new day, full of possibilities.

Since then, I have learned that joy comes in the *mourning* as well. God wants to turn our wailing into dancing (see Ps. 30:11) and to replace our mourning with the oil of gladness, which results in everlasting joy (see Isa. 61:3,7).

Jeremiah looked ahead to the time when the Messiah would establish the Kingdom. He prophesied: "Then maidens will dance and be glad, young men and old as well. I will turn their mourning into gladness; I will give them comfort and joy instead of sorrow" (Jer. 31:13).

Jesus promises, "Hugely happy (*makarios*) are you who weep now, for you will laugh" (see Luke 6:21). When? When the Kingdom comes. Of course, Jesus proclaimed that the Kingdom of God is near (or "at hand" in the NASB) (see Matt. 4:17).

When my daughter cries over a disappointment that she has experienced, I try my best to comfort her. Sometimes I will just sit with her, ready to listen. I do not go into her room and say, "Oh, you're crying, way to go. Crying is so good for you. I am so happy for you. Keep it up!" No, I do my best to lead her into a smile and a laugh at some point.

Sometimes it may take me a little while to change her mood, but that is my goal; I desire to see my daughter smiling and laughing. I want to see her happy. It is normal for me as a father to want her to be happy.

Our heavenly Father is the same. He is a good father who desires happiness for His children. Sure, He will comfort us in our pain and sorrow, but His intent is to bring our mood into alignment with His. God is in a good mood. He is in Heaven laughing, and He wants the same for us.

As previously mentioned, when the angel came to announce the birth of Jesus, the message was, "Do not be afraid. I bring you good news of great joy that will be for all the people" (Luke 2:10).

Notice, the angel did not say, "You should be afraid because I have some really bad news that is going to make you depressed for life!" No, Jesus came to replace hopelessness and depression with everlasting joy, to substitute mourning for the oil of gladness (see Isa. 61:3,7). He came to change the atmosphere. He came to bring a party!

LET'S PARTY

In Psalm 2:4, David observes: "The One enthroned in heaven laughs...." The context, of course, is that God looks at the strategies of those who are against God's people and laughs. When God sees the enemy plotting evil for us, He does not break down and cry in hopelessness; no, He laughs because He has the answer; He *is* the answer!

Therefore, as kids of the King, we do not have to be ruled by fear and hopelessness. We can confidently laugh in the face of trials, sickness, and even death, knowing that God has a supernatural solution for every problem we face.

In Psalm 23:4, David describes traveling through the valley of the shadow of death. He says, "...I will fear no evil, for you are with me...." In other words, when God is with us, who can be against us? No one. The good news is that Jesus promised that He would be with us always, to the very end of the age (see Matt. 28:20).

David goes on in the next verse to describe how God has prepared a table before him in the presence of his enemies (see Ps. 23:5). When armies would fight battles in those days, the victor would set up tables on the battlefield and throw a party of celebration, consuming the spoils that they had retrieved from the enemy's camp or city.

David is comforted by the fact that God sets up the victory party before the battle is even fought. In other words, God is so confident in His ability to win any battle that He can celebrate, even in the face of the most intimidating and formidable foe.

While I was in San Diego, conducting a Firestorm conference, a man approached me at the end of one of the meetings, asking if I ever went after creative miracles. "Absolutely," I replied.

He held up his left hand, revealing half of a thumb. He explained that he had cut it off with a skill saw several years prior.

Without saying anything else, I grabbed his thumb and began to laugh. About five minutes later, as I was actually praying over someone else at the same time, I let go of his thumb. In shock, we both stared at the brand-new thumb that had grown while I held his half-thumb in my hand and laughed.

He began showing it to those around, and we noticed that he still did not have a thumbnail. I called three of our Supernatural Ministry students over and instructed them to give him a new thumbnail. Without hesitation, they surrounded him and began to laugh. Shortly after, the beginning of a thumbnail emerged. Obviously we were all extremely ecstatic and could not contain our exuberant joy. There were no golf-claps.

When I encounter God's presence, experiencing fullness of joy, I can look at missing limbs, cancer, auto immune deficiencies, blood disorders, diseases, ailments, and disorders of any kind and laugh, knowing that God has already set up the victory celebration and is laughing at the foolishness of the enemy's plans. I can laugh with joy, knowing that God is with me and that impossibilities bow to His presence!

LAUGHTER HEALS LUPUS

Prior to speaking at a conference a few months ago, God gave me the name "Rhonda" and the word "lupus" as a word of knowledge that I wrote down on my teaching notes. Before I began to launch into the subject that I was teaching that evening, I asked if a Rhonda was present. I asked a few times, but no one responded, so I went on with my message, wondering why Rhonda had not responded.

About ten minutes into my teaching, however, I could not get "Rhonda" off my mind, so I stopped to ask one more time, "There has to be a Rhonda here—is there a Rhonda here?"

One of the elders, sitting in the second row, sheepishly raised his hand and confessed that his wife was named Rhonda, but that she was at home sick.

"Get her on the cell phone," I insisted.

Once he got her on the phone, he handed the phone to me. I introduced myself and explained the word of knowledge that I had received prior to the meeting.

I asked if there was a possibility that she had lupus. At that, she burst into tears, along with her husband in the second row. As she continued crying over the phone, her husband explained to the congregation that Rhonda had been diagnosed with lupus that very week and was at home in terrible pain. She had not told anyone in the church because she was so depressed over the prognosis that she would never recover—there was no cure.

I began to share with Rhonda that God had a different prognosis, that He had highlighted her to show her that He wanted to heal her. With that knowledge, she began to laugh hysterically through the cell phone, which prompted me to laugh. I put her on speakerphone, and as her laughter belted into the auditorium, the entire congregation erupted in spontaneous laughter.

After laughing for about ten minutes, I asked how she was feeling. Through bursts of laughter, she shared that all of the pain had left, starting with her arms and finishing with her legs. She was completely healed.

The next morning, she came to both church services to testify of the healing and demonstrate her glowing countenance. She also shared that she and her husband had spent a few hours laughing together upon his return that night. When the Kingdom shows up, there is joy and anything is possible.

GOD IS IN A GOOD MOOD

I have a picture on a shelf in my office depicting Jesus laughing, which constantly reminds me of His mood toward me. Throughout the day, as I happen to glance at it, I am overwhelmed with a sense of supernatural strengthening as I remember that "...the joy of the Lord is my strength" (Neh. 8:10). In other words, when we encounter His joy, an empowering comes, not only internally, but also in the releasing of miracles.

God is in a good mood. Moreover, when we are able to picture His good mood toward us, it releases the supernatural Kingdom in and through our lives. Furthermore, we tend to minister to the people around us out of the view that we have of God.

I have learned that, as I operate out of His supernatural joy, I am filled with supernatural power that can heal the sick and set the captives free. In First Chronicles 16:27, David proclaims, "Splendor and majesty are before Him; strength and joy are in His dwelling place." If we desire to be empowered to live naturally supernatural lives, it is imperative that we live from His presence, where we find the supernatural power of overflowing joy.

Recently, while speaking at a conference, I was approached by a middle-aged man who had been born deaf in his right ear. I had finished speaking and was signing books in the foyer. He asked if I could pray for him and knelt down next to where I was sitting.

I began to laugh as the joy of the Lord flooded my spirit at the thought of this man being able to hear out of his ear for the first time in his life. I placed my hand on his deaf ear and immediately felt an electric heat sensation in the palm of my hand. I continued laughing for the next few minutes as I kept my electrified hand on his ear.

I then asked him to plug his good ear with his finger, close his eyes, and lift his right hand when he heard me snap my fingers. On the third snap, he raised his hand. I pulled my hand back farther and farther, as I continued to snap at different intervals, until my hand was completely extended.

He was absolutely shocked when he opened his eyes to find that the snapping sound was so far away. He stood up and walked about 15 feet away to do further testing. Each time I snapped my fingers, he raised his hand. He went farther into the auditorium, where a party was still going on with music and dancing. Again he raised his hand in response to the snapping. At that, he ran back to me, weeping with tears of joy, utterly amazed that he had just been healed!

Focusing on God's joy is a crucial Kingdom key to unlocking Heaven and living a naturally supernatural life. Moreover, when we spend time in His presence (His dwelling place), we avail ourselves of the power that comes through "drinking and leaking," which we will discuss in the next chapter.

ENDNOTES

1. W.E. Vine, *Vine's Expository Dictionary of New Testament Words* (McLean, VA: MacDonald Publishing Company, n.d.), 134-135.

2. Gerhard Kittle, *Theological Dictionary of the New Testament,* vol. 4 (Grand Rapids, MI: Eerdmans, 1964), 362-370.

Chapter 6

DRINKING AND LEAKING

I have three mandatory requirements when students from our Bethel School of Supernatural Ministry travel with me as I go to speak at a church or conference. The first rule is that they must get "drunk" in the Holy Spirit before we leave. The second rule is that they must stay drunk through the duration of the trip. The third rule is that they must get others drunk.

The reason for these requirements is that drunken people take more risks than sober people do. For example, people drunk on alcohol will sing in public, even if they cannot sing well. Drunks will say anything to anyone, even if the other person does not want to listen. They will even jump off of a cliff into water that is too shallow. They do crazy things because they are drunk!

Likewise, Holy Spirit-drunk Christians take more risks than "sober" Christians do. For example, drunken Christians will prophesy over strangers, even though they would normally feel intimidated and incompetent. Drunken Christians will pray for someone in a wheelchair at a supermarket, even though they may not feel "gifted" in healing. They just do not care about what others think of them. They have lost all fear of man and fear of failure. They will try just about anything.

In Ephesians 5:18, the apostle Paul warns, "Do not get drunk on wine, which leads to debauchery. Instead, be filled with the Spirit." In other words, get drunk in the Spirit and stay drunk in the Spirit. I call this L.U.I.: Living Under the Influence.

The Greek verb for "be filled" in Ephesians 5:18 is in the present tense, which in the Greek language has an ongoing, continuous sense. The present tense in Greek has the connotation of doing something over and over. So when Paul commands the Ephesians to be filled with the Spirit, he is instructing them to do it every day—to live under the influence.

Being filled with the Spirit is contrasted with being drunk on the wine of the world. Paul is telling them to be drunk, but not with wine, which leads to debauchery.

Debauchery means losing all of your inhibitions so that you do things—evil and wicked things—that you are ashamed of, and usually sorry for, the next day. In other words, when you drink the wine of the world, you lose all inhibition (fear), which allows you to take crazy risks. The problem is that, once you sober up, sadness follows as you contemplate why you did what you did.

Conversely, when we are drunk with the Spirit, we lose our inhibitions (fear), which enables us to take crazy risks, leading toward acts of righteousness through which people are healed, saved, and set free. Furthermore, the next day, we are very proud of what happened as a result of our drunkenness.

I normally have the ministry team that is traveling with me begin their journey at our church's Prayer House. We gather together to laugh and take communion, drinking in God's presence in preparation, getting ready to leak on those we meet who may need a miracle. The goal is to continue drinking through the duration of the trip, knowing that we could have a divine appointment anywhere and at anytime along the way.

On one occasion, as we were making our way home, we stopped at a mini-mart in the middle of nowhere, north of Sacramento, California. Amazingly, even at 10:00 P.M., after a weekend of intense ministry and a very long drive, the team piled out of the van, still laughing and enjoying God's presence. They were still drinking.

As I was pumping gas, I saw my wife with two of our team praying for three people next to the entrance to the mini-mart. Before long, they were testing out knees and backs to confirm the healings they had experienced when my wife and the students leaked God's presence onto them by laying hands on them.

Meanwhile, over by the restroom, a few more students had a trucker bending over and touching his toes to confirm that he had been healed. As it turned out, he had told his driving partner that he could not drive anymore because his back was hurting so badly. They had decided to stop at the mini-mart to get something cold to drink and to stretch.

As soon as they got out of the truck, one of our students received a word of knowledge, sensing pain in someone's back. Drunk in the Spirit, the student looked over at the trucker and asked if he had any pain in his back. Shocked, the trucker asked how the student could have known and told of his reason for pulling into the mini-mart. He was then healed.

Another team was inside the mini-mart, and instinctively, I knew what was going on with them because, whenever our students drink, they just naturally take risks and reach out to people wherever they can find them. They do not need an outreach event; they *are* an outreach wherever they go. They just cannot help but leak.

Just then, a woman with a mini-mart uniform came out with a concerned look on her face. She spotted me and immediately began walking toward me. My first thought was, *Oh great, here we go. She is probably mad about the revival that has just broken out in her mini-mart.*

As she reached me, she asked if I was the leader of the group who had just invaded her mini-mart. I sheepishly responded in the affirmative, bracing myself for a rebuke. To my surprise, however, she was not mad at all. Still, with a concerned look on her face, she related her reason for approaching me.

She explained that she had been to the doctor that morning and had been informed that she had cervical cancer. She had a husband and two young girls and could not muster the courage to tell them. Her shift was nearly over, and she did not know how she was going to break the bad news. Even though she was not a Christian, when she saw all of the people being healed in and outside of the mini-mart, she began to think that we could help her.

She went on to say that she did not want to say anything inside the store because a local could come in and overhear the conversation and possibly leak the information to her family before she had the courage to tell them herself. With that in mind, she had asked where the leader of our group was, and the students inside directed her to me.

I called Becky, one of our students, over to help me minister to the woman, and we immediately began to call out her destiny through prophetic words. We then began to pray for her with laughter and proclamations of God's goodness. After a few minutes, she looked up with tear-soaked eyes and explained that she had felt "butterfly" sensations going through her cervix. After we were done blessing her, she thanked us profusely for stopping at her mini-mart.

WE ARE NOT DRUNK AS YOU SUPPOSE

In Acts 2, the Holy Spirit is poured out on the Church, and the disciples are filled (see Acts 2:1-4). The crowd that has gathered around to observe the happenings of the event begins to accuse the disciples of being drunk. Obviously, they must have displayed some manifestations that led to that conclusion.

Peter's response, however, is, "These men are not drunk as you suppose..." (Acts 2:15). Notice that he is not denying the fact that they are drunk; rather, he is denying that they are drunk in the way that the others think they are drunk (with wine). Peter explains:

This is what was spoken by the prophet Joel: "In the last days, God says, I will pour out My Spirit on all people..." (Acts 2:16-17).

Peter's explanation of their drunken behavior is that the Spirit of God has come upon them. They have been filled with the Spirit, and they are drunk with the new wine from Heaven, which is available to anyone who wants it.

Peter expands on this invitation, pointing out that the new wine (the Spirit) is only distributed through Jesus. By verse 37, the people ask, "Brothers, what shall we do?" They obviously want to get the same wine that the disciples have. So Peter instructs them, in the next verse, to repent and be baptized, and 3,000 people get saved!

What an amazing response to Peter's first attempt at preaching. Moreover, this same Peter, who denied Jesus three times because he was gripped by fear, now stands up and fearlessly addresses a mocking crowd that is potentially very dangerous (further proof that drunken people take more risks than sober people).

For me, the more I drink in the Holy Spirit, the more confident and bold I become in taking radical risks. I find that I become amazingly uninhibited as I am filled with His empowering presence. I will prophesy over strangers in public places and pray for people with seemingly hopeless physical conditions when I am drunk. Sober, I am more apt to pass an opportunity by than to take a risk in order to release the Kingdom. Drinking and leaking are vital keys to living a naturally supernatural life.

You Were Intended to Leak

Interestingly, after the disciples are filled in Acts 2:1-4, without any explanation or transition verse, they are transported from the upper room to the community outside. It is God's intention that we have an encounter so that others can have an encounter. In other words, it is our objective to be filled with the Spirit and then to leak what we have consumed.

Jesus describes this dynamic in John 7:37-38:

If anyone is thirsty, let him come to Me and drink. Whoever believes in Me, as the Scripture has said, streams of living water will flow from within him.

John explains, "By this He meant the Spirit, whom those who believed in Him were later to receive..." (John 7:39). Jesus wants us to get drunk, to stay drunk, and to get others drunk. He invites those who are thirsty for new wine, for the Spirit, to come and drink to overflowing. His intention is that we drink and leak.

This is a fulfillment of the prophetic picture found in Ezekiel 47:1-12. There we find a description of how the river (streams of living water) develops and what it accomplishes as it flows (from within us) to the thirsty.

Ezekiel writes:

The man brought me back to the entrance of the temple, and I saw water coming out from under the threshold of the temple toward the east (for the temple faced east). The water was coming down from under the south side of the temple, south of the altar. He then brought me out through the north gate and led me around the outside to the outer gate facing east, and the water was flowing from the south side.

As the man went eastward with a measuring line in his hand, he measured off a thousand cubits and then led me through water that was ankle-deep. He measured off another thousand cubits and led me through water that was knee-deep. He measured off another thousand and led me through water that was up to the waist. He measured off another thousand, but now it was a river that I could not cross, because the water had risen and was deep enough to swim in—a river that no one could cross. He asked me, "Son of man, do you see this?"

Then he led me back to the bank of the river. When I arrived there, I saw a great number of trees on each side of the river. He said to me, "This water flows toward the eastern region and goes down into the Arabah, where it enters the Sea. When it empties into the Sea, the water there becomes fresh. Swarms of living creatures will live wherever the river flows. There will be large numbers of fish, because this water flows there and makes the salt water fresh; so where the river flows everything will live. Fishermen will stand along the shore; from En Gedi to En Eglaim there will be places for spreading nets. The fish will be of many kinds—like the fish of the Great Sea. But the swamps and marshes will not become fresh; they will be left for salt. Fruit trees of all kinds will grow on both banks of the river. Their leaves will not wither, nor will their fruit fail. Every month they will bear, because the water from the sanctuary flows to them. Their fruit will serve for food and their leaves for healing."

Notice that the river originates at the south side of the temple, south of the altar. This is the location in the temple where the priests would offer up worship to the Lord. It is a picture of drinking in God's presence through worship, praise, and thanksgiving, resulting in joy and happiness and manifesting in laughter and the release of the supernatural.

As discussed in the previous chapter, fullness of joy is found in His presence (see Ps. 16:11). This river pictured by Ezekiel, and the corresponding streams of living water described by Jesus, is the joy that originates in God's presence. It is a river of joy in the Holy Spirit.

Moreover, this joy (an expression of God's presence through His Spirit) grows in increasing measure as it is solely connected to the place of worship (be continually filled with the Spirit). As we continue to drink, we are more and more filled to overflowing so that we are able to bring healing and life to those around us.

A GREETING OF LAUGHTER

During the time of worship at a church where I had been invited to speak, a woman came through a door to the right of the stage. She was hooked up to an oxygen tank on wheels, which her husband was pushing behind her, and she was followed by her three children, walking in single file.

It took what seemed like forever for her to make it halfway to the front row, where I was sitting with the ministry team that I had brought. She was struggling at each step, and I found myself rooting for her to make it to a chair. By the time she got to the crowded front row, I could not bear watching her labor any longer. I offered our seats, which she and her family gladly accepted, and I stood next to her on the end seat, continuing to worship.

I had been drinking all morning, and as I stood next to the woman, I began to leak. Without any greeting, without even knowing what was wrong with her, I put my hand on her head and spontaneously erupted into laughter. This is not the way that I normally begin a time of ministry, but because I was drunk, I lost all sense of protocol.

Immediately I could feel her head bobbing up and down as she began laughing hysterically. We continued to laugh, still without a proper introduction. After a few minutes, she jumped out of her chair, pulled the oxygen hoses out of her nostrils, and sucked in the atmosphere, filling her lungs to capacity.

She breathed out the air that she had inhaled and looked at me with surprise. Not knowing her medical condition, I gave her a look like, "OK, you can breathe—that's good...." Knowing that I did not understand the significance of her breathing feat, she explained that she had not been able to breathe like that in years.

She further explained that she had been in and out of hospitals over the past few years and that she had almost died several times. Moreover, even though she had gone to specialist after specialist, no one could diagnose the problem. Out of frustration, they finally termed her condition "a failure to thrive."

She had racked up over a million dollars in co-payments alone, and she still had no hope for breakthrough. The day before she came to church, she had been released from the hospital, where she had been treated for a severe case of pneumonia, the effects of which she was still suffering from. She was supposed to be on complete bed-rest, but she had felt like she just had to get to church that morning.

She ran over to the pastors and repeated the same breathing demonstration she had performed for me. The pastors looked on with wide eyes of excitement as the woman took off running across the front of the auditorium.

She then picked up a flag and began running, jumping, and dancing to the roar of the congregation, who all were quite aware of her medical condition. I found out later that most of the church had been taking turns caring for her and her family over the previous two years with meals, housekeeping, and emotional support.

The pastor finally had her share her testimony, in which she exclaimed that all of the pain in her body had left and that her lungs had been completely restored. Six months later, the husband sent word through the pastor, thanking me for leaking on his wife because they now have their lives back!

That is the supernatural power of drinking and leaking.

OVERFLOWING, LEAKING JOY

In John 17, Jesus prays six things for the disciples. He prays that they will be protected (see John 17:11,15), that they will be sanctified (see John 17:17-19), that they will be unified (see John 17:20-23), that they will have His glory (see John 17:24), that they will experience His presence (see John 17:24), and that they will encounter His love (see John 17:26).

In verse 13, Jesus prays, "I say all of these things [the six things He is praying in the chapter]...so that they may have the full measure of My joy within them." The goal of being sanctified, protected, and unified, of having God's glory and experiencing His presence and love, is that we will have all of the joy that Jesus carries.

The question is: how much joy does Jesus have? How much is a "full measure"? Does He just have enough for one person, one event, or one circumstance? Does He just have enough for one season of life? Is His measure equivalent to a gallon, a water truck, a lake, or an ocean?

Jesus' joy is limitless. His joy is eternal, everlasting. Therefore, it is immeasurable. A full measure of Jesus' joy will never run out. There is a constant supply. This is the very measure that Jesus is praying would be in us—an unending, limitless, everlasting supply of joy.

So then, what happens when His container of immeasurable joy flows into us? We will be able to say with David, in Psalm 23:5, "My cup overflows." Imagine God's limitless measure of joy as a liter-sized bottle, and imagine your container size, designed to hold this joy, as the cap. What would happen if you poured the liter measure into the cap? It would run over.

When His limitless measure comes into our finite container, it naturally overflows. We cannot contain the full measure of God's joy; it must leak out of us like streams of living water.

Jesus prayed that we would have so much joy that, wherever we went, we would leak on everyone around us. This is one of the keys to releasing the Kingdom of God; it is a key to living a naturally supernatural life. Drinking and leaking God's presence, His joy, can literally change the world around us.

I was in India recently. We visited a place where 30 million Hindus gather over a two-week span to worship various gods. We were told not to witness about Jesus, since violence has been known to break out against those who do.

Instead, we just leaked the presence of God in the middle of all of the Hindus worshiping their gods. We preached without using words as we laughed, leaking His presence into the atmosphere. Soon, a Hindu man approached me and, grabbing my hands, began to laugh along with me. We held hands laughing for a few minutes, and then he began saying through his laughter, "Thank you! Thank you!" over and over.

He could sense something different in me, and even though we could not communicate verbally, he got the message. We ended up taking photographs with many of the Hindus who were gathered because they were attracted to the joy leaking out of us.

We can change the atmosphere around us as God's full measure of joy—His presence—leaks out of us wherever we go. Francis of Assisi once said, "Preach the Gospel all the time. If necessary, use words."[1] People all around are waiting for you to leak on them the joy of Heaven.

"You Want Some of This?"

I'll never forget one time when I stopped for gas on a ministry trip and our ministry team fell out of the van, thoroughly drunk. They eventually ended up in a heap between the gas pump islands. As I was pumping gas, I noticed a man pumping gas directly across from me. I instantly wondered what he might be thinking as he stared at the pile of laughing students having a great party in the middle of the gas station.

Just then, one of our students caught the man's eye and asked, "You want some of this?"

The man instantly nodded yes.

The student followed up and asked, "Do you know what this is?"

The man slowly shook his head no.

The student then invited the man over, promptly leading him to Christ and getting him filled with the Spirit. The man finally drove away laughing with the joy of the Lord! That was an amazing demonstration of the Kingdom principle of drinking and leaking.

As mentioned earlier, in Acts 2, on the day of Pentecost, the disciples drank until they overflowed. Both then and now, people are thirsty for the water from Heaven. They are thirsty for a real encounter with a good God who is in a good mood and who demonstrates His goodness and good mood through laughter, signs and wonders, miracles, healings, and prophetic insights that call out the gold in people.

How Long Is This Going to Last?

Sometimes I will gather a few friends for a guys' night out of drinking and leaking. We will usually start out at the In-N-Out Burger (the closest restaurant to Heaven on earth that I have found) and then allow the Lord to direct us to leak somewhere.

On this particular occasion, we were drinking while eating our "Double-Double" hamburgers and fries. We prayed for a few people there in the restaurant, and then we decided to head over to the hospital.

After visiting a patient we knew from church, we decided to head over to the Emergency Room waiting room. I like going there because you do not have to look long to find someone who needs to be healed.

As I entered the room, I announced, "If you don't want to wait for the doctor, we can take care of you now. We are Christians, and we see a lot of people healed when we pray." As usual, we were met with skeptical looks, so we began to prophesy the secrets of their hearts and call out words of knowledge for the ailments that they were suffering from.

After about 20 minutes of building rapport with those waiting for medical treatment, we invited anyone who wanted our services to come outside, where we would be waiting. Soon people started coming out, asking for prayer.

A woman suffering from endometriosis approached two of my friends who had formed a makeshift healing office on a bench. My other friend and I were ministering nearby to a young woman with scoliosis.

After we had seen a good amount of breakthrough on the young woman with scoliosis, we turned our attention to the woman with endometriosis, who was in the process of being dramatically healed. In shock, she announced that all of the pain had left. She then asked Jesus into her heart and began to laugh uncontrollably as the presence of God inundated her.

After about ten minutes, doubled over, she looked up and asked, "How long is this [the laughter] going to last?"

My immediate response was, "I hope forever!"

She laughed more at that and was still laughing when we finally had to head for home.

When we drink and leak, anything is possible. The atmosphere is affected when the Kingdom is released through our joy, and people are healed, saved, and set free. Furthermore, when the river overflows through our lives, carrying signs and wonders, miracles, healing, and prophetic insights, the salt water is transformed into joyous life.

God wants us to have an encounter so that we can become an encounter so that others can have an encounter. He wants us to drink and leak wherever we go, releasing His supernatural Kingdom river to everyone who is thirsty for the living waters of Heaven.

A classic example of this phenomenon is described in Acts 8, when Philip goes to Samaria to preach the Good News. Once everyone there had encountered God's goodness, demonstrated in miraculous healings, they believed in Jesus, and there was great joy in that city (see Acts 8:5-8).

As stated earlier, the Kingdom is released through joy—His presence. When we are carriers of His presence, we become a conduit of His presence, distributing His presence according to the measure that we have drunk in His Spirit.

The level of joy in a city should be commensurate with the amount of the Kingdom demonstrated. Our drinking should have a positive effect on the community around us, resulting in joy wherever we go.

FULFILLING THE IMPOSSIBLE MISSION

We are called to be revivalist (world-changer) history makers. We are God's chosen vessels, through whom, in His sovereignty, He has chosen to reveal His goodness. Ours is an amazing calling and destiny, which can often feel overwhelming to fulfill.

When Abraham and Sarah were given the promise that a nation would be birthed through them, even though they were way past their ability to have children, they laughed at the notion (see Gen. 17:17; 18:12). I believe they laughed (got drunk) because they knew that they could not bring about their destiny.

Notice, God does not scold them for laughing. In Sarah's case, God simply points out that she laughed. Even when Sarah denies it, there is no punishment or correction, just an acknowledgement of the laughter in the face of the impossibility (see Gen. 18:13-15). Conversely, God does not even mention Abraham's laughter in response to the impossible destiny that he was to fulfill.

In fact, they were both inducted into the Hall of Faith in Hebrews 11 for believing against all odds. The apostle Paul states: "Abraham believed God, and it was credited to him as righteousness" (see Rom. 4:3).

He then goes on in verses 18-22:

Against all hope, Abraham in hope believed and so became the father of many nations, just as it had been said to him.... Without weakening in his faith, he faced the fact that his body was as good as dead—since he was about a hundred years old—and Sarah's womb was also dead. Yet he did not waver through unbelief regarding the promise of God, but was strengthened in his faith and gave glory to God, being fully persuaded that God had power to do what he had promised. This is why "it was credited to him as righteousness."

It seems that laughter is an appropriate response to impossible promises and circumstances. Moreover, I believe that laughter is a primary key that unlocks Heaven and releases the Kingdom in and through our lives.

We have been called to represent (re-present) the King and His Kingdom, which can feel overwhelming. I think the disciples felt the same way when Jesus announced that they were going to make disciples of all nations (see Matt. 28:19). I can imagine the conversations they had in the upper room as they contemplated the impossibility of the mission.

Getting drunk on the day of Pentecost, however, changed their perspective on what God could do in and through them. They found that drinking and leaking were keys to their success in releasing the Kingdom wherever they went. In Acts 13:52, Luke describes the constant condition of the believers: "The disciples were filled with joy and the Holy Spirit."

If the apostles needed to get drunk, and stay drunk, to accomplish their mission, then how much more do we need to be continually filled with joy and the Holy Spirit to fulfill our mission? We have been called to do the impossible—to walk in signs and wonders and miracles. We cannot do it on our own.

We must have a higher source of power operating in and through our lives. That source is God's presence, where there is fullness of joy. A river does not work to bring the water into the valleys. It simply flows from a higher source. In the same way, releasing the Kingdom means simply allowing the river of joy to flow through us from Heaven; it is bringing Heaven to earth. To that end, the best way to live a naturally supernatural life—to fulfill the impossible mission—is to cultivate a lifestyle of drinking and leaking.

ENDNOTE

1. "Saint Francis of Assisi," http://www.giga-usa.com/quotes /authors/francis_1_a001.htm (accessed Dec. 30, 2008).

Chapter 7

INHALING AND EXHALING

I once had a vision in which I found myself standing in the front passenger's side of a 1965 Chevrolet Impala two-door convertible traveling down a country road with Jesus at the wheel. Leaning against the windshield, with hands outstretched to the sides, and hair blowing in the wind, I felt like Leonardo DiCaprio in the movie, *Titanic*.

In the vision, I could almost feel the wind in my face as I experienced exhilaration like I had never encountered before. I felt both empowered and free. It was like I could go anywhere and do anything I wanted. Standing in the wind made the drive fun and refreshing, causing me to feel completely renewed in body, soul, and spirit.

Immediately I realized that this is the way God intends for me to release the Kingdom. The road represents my life adventure. The car represents my life in God.

I instantly knew that a key to living a naturally supernatural life was operating in an open heaven (the convertible) where I commune with God in intimacy (finding rest and restoration) as the Spirit (the wind) breathes life on me and enables me to live in the freedom of Jesus' will (Jesus at the wheel).

In the vision, I sensed an invitation to the Church to put the top down—to remove any religious hindrances or self-created obstacles that would prevent us from communing with God. There is a call to minister out of intimacy in these days—to drive in an open heaven in which we are continually empowered and refreshed, not to mention having fun in the process.

THE WORD AND THE WIND

As I was basking in this scene, the vision suddenly changed. All of a sudden, a lion appeared, sitting on his haunches in front of me. Instantly, I knew that it was not a ferocious, killing lion, but a lion similar to Aslan in *The Chronicles of Narnia*. It was the Lion of the tribe of Judah (see Rev. 5:5)—Jesus, the lion of praise and worship.

As I stared at the beauty and strength of the lion (Jesus), he opened his mouth and began to breathe on me. As in the vision of the convertible, my hair blew back from the wind of his breath, and I felt more alive than ever before.

Suddenly, the breath coming toward me went into slow motion and became magnified so that I could see every particle within the breath. Within seconds, the scene shifted again, and the particles slowed down further and magnified to twice their previous size, enabling me to see that each particle in the breath of the lion was a word—a name of God—the Word of God.

A continuous, unending flow of the Word of God crept toward me, representing all of the various names of God. Each name represented in the lion's breath described His nature, character, personality, and attributes. For example, *peace* came out of his mouth, as did *counsel, wisdom, abundance, comfort, healing, joy, salvation,* and so forth. As the particles came toward me, I could sense the inherent power in each one of the words (the names of God).

John, the apostle, identifies Jesus as the *Logos*, referring to Him as the Word (*Logos*) of God (*Theos*)—the full expression and manifestation of God (see John 1:1-14). Jesus, therefore, perfectly communicates, embodies, and demonstrates the nature, character, personality, and attributes of God the Father.

The Greek word *logos* originated in Alexandrian times and simply referred to "speech, communication, or an utterance" in the classical Greek language. *Logos* also embodied the creativity, logic, ideas, and reason underlying the speech, communication, or utterance, as well as the effects of whatever was communicated.[1]

Later, in Greek philosophy, the *Logos* (the Word) was additionally defined as the full expression of God (*Theos*)—the Word of God. The Greeks, of course, believed in many gods, but the highest, most supreme "god" was the *Logos*, the Word, which empowered all of the others.

The *Logos* represented everything that God was communicating and was considered to be the supreme source of all creativity, reason, power, and will in the universe; it was the underlying, unseen force responsible for everything created. Even thoughts, ideas, and inventions were communicated by and caught from this invisible realm in which the *Logos* originated.[2]

John then, in his Gospel account, proclaims Jesus as the visible, physical manifestation of God when he points out, "The Word became flesh and made His dwelling among us. We have seen His glory, the glory of the One and Only, who came from the Father, full of grace and truth" (John 1:14).

Interestingly, the Greek word translated "grace" (*charis*) carries the connotation of "empowerment" (see Rom. 1:5; 12:6; 15:15; 1 Cor. 3:10; Gal. 2:9; Eph. 3:2,7).[3] In other words, Jesus, the Word (*Logos*) of God, came to empower us as He communicated the Father's will through the breath of the Holy Spirit.

To that end, in my vision, as the particles (the Word of God) came closer, I opened my mouth to receive the breath (the Holy Spirit). I could see each particle coming toward my mouth and then disappearing inside. Each time a particle entered my mouth, I immediately felt the effects of the meaning of the word—an aspect of His name. I felt the empowerment—the grace—inherent in each word that I received from the lion.

As *joy* entered me, for example, I felt the exuberant joy of Heaven. When *peace* entered, I had a peace that went beyond understanding. I could feel His presence healing every ailment as *healing* entered. I felt totally secure as *love* entered. On and on it went until I had received all of the Word of God—the names of God in the breath. I soon realized that everything that I needed was contained in the lion's breath.

Later I discovered that breath does carry particles and that they are passed on. Whatever is inside the person breathing is given to those who breathe in that air. That is why it is not appropriate to breathe on someone when you are sick! You give them what you have.

In the same way, when God breathes on us, we get whatever He has. In His case, it is healthy and brings life to the recipient. In other words, whatever God breathes on us, we become.

In the vision, the lion represents Jesus, the Word of God. The breath (the wind) represents the Holy Spirit, which empowers the Word. Thus, we need both the Word and the Wind in order for us to live naturally supernatural lives.

I have found that, whenever I enter into a place of praise before the Lion of the tribe of Judah, I encounter an open heaven. In that environment, in the secret place of His presence, I receive the Word and the Wind, which carries everything that I need from God, leaving me satisfied, fulfilled, renewed, encouraged, and strengthened.

We need both the Word and the Wind in order to live the supernatural life that we have been called to. We need the living Word of God speaking life into our circumstances, needs, and destiny. We need the life-giving breath of God to empower those words to work their full effect.

We have been called to represent the Kingdom of God on earth, which can sometimes feel impossible to accomplish. For me, I know that I need more of the Word and Wind every day if I expect to live in my destiny as a revivalist and world-changer.

BREATHE IN, BREATHE OUT

Often, when I share this vision, I will release an impartation to the audience. I will breathe on them as a prophetic act to release what they need from His presence. As a result, I have seen many people healed as I have prophesied breath into those who need a breakthrough miracle.

I remember one woman who had had fibromyalgia for 15 years. She was in such constant pain that she could barely function during the day or sleep through the night. After receiving the impartation of the lion's breath, she began to notice that the pain throughout her body was decreasing, and she felt energy flowing into her limbs.

She came back the next day and reported that she had actually overslept. She had slept through the entire night without waking once, and she had not taken her usual dose of pain medication and sleep aids.

She also reported that, when she woke up the next morning, she immediately got out of bed and began doing household chores. In the process of doing her morning's work, she suddenly realized that it usually took her two hours to just start moving around due to the normal stiffness she experienced from a pain-filled, restless night. She was completely healed as the Word and the Wind blew on her the night before!

I have also had reports of people receiving freedom from fears, release into joy, wisdom for a decision, comfort, encouragement, and so on as I have released the breath of God onto them. When God breathes His supernatural breath on us, anything is possible.

Unfortunately, most Christians stop right there. They inhale what they need from God's presence, and stingily keep all of it to themselves. That is where "renewal" can fall short of God's ultimate purpose. God intends for us to breathe out what we have breathed in. We were designed to inhale and exhale. This is the simple secret of living a naturally supernatural life.

Let's hope, in the natural, that no one has to remind themselves to take a breath and then to exhale. The act of breathing should be a natural exercise that should require no thought. You have to think about *not* doing it. Similarly, it should be natural for us to inhale His presence and then to exhale His presence on those around us who need His miraculous power.

In fact, if we do not exhale what we have inhaled, we will die. What started out as life, if it is not given away, will result in death. Renewal is breathing in. Revival is breathing out. We need both to live a naturally supernatural life.

Fortunately, my experience of inhaling the Word and the Wind was not the end of my vision. Just as naturally as I had received the breath into my lungs, I desired to exhale—to give it away.

In the continuing vision, I turned around and saw a great multitude of people with mouths wide open, gasping for air. As I breathed out what I had inhaled—the names of God—I saw those very names coming out of my mouth in slow motion and magnified to those in the crowd.

I saw *joy* go into one person's mouth, and immediately she began to dance and laugh with fullness of joy. *Peace* entered another person's mouth. *Wisdom, counsel, abundance, acceptance, healing, deliverance, salvation*—whatever the person needed, the breath brought the very characteristic of God's name that would meet the need and desire.

I immediately knew that this was the way that we could change the world. This is a true picture of revival. This is bringing Heaven to earth. This is living a naturally supernatural life.

PROPHESY TO THE BONES

Not only *can* we change the world, bringing Heaven to earth, but we also have a responsibility to *do* so. We have a responsibility to exhale whatever we have inhaled from His presence. The world is waiting for us to breathe on them.

In Ezekiel 37:1-10, Ezekiel shares a vision of a revival lifestyle:

The hand of the Lord was on me, and He brought me out by the Spirit of the Lord and set me in the middle of a valley; it was full of bones. He led me back and forth among them, and I saw a great many bones on the floor of the valley, bones that were very dry. He asked me, "Son of man, can these bones live?"

I said, "O sovereign Lord, You alone know."

Then He said to me, "Prophesy to these bones and say to them, 'Dry bones, hear the word of the Lord! This is what the Sovereign Lord says to these bones: I will make breath enter you, and you will come to life. I will attach tendons to you and make flesh come upon you and cover you with skin; I will put breath in you, and you will come to life. Then you will know that I am the Lord.'"

So I prophesied as I was commanded. And as I was prophesying, there was a noise, a rattling sound, and the bones came together, bone to bone. I looked, and tendons and flesh appeared on them and skin covered them, but there was no breath in them.

Then He said to me, "Prophesy to the breath; prophesy, son of man, and say to it, 'This is what the Sovereign Lord says: Come from the four winds, O breath, and breathe into these slain, that they may live.'" So I prophesied as He commanded me, and breath entered them; they came to life and stood up on their feet—a vast army.

Notice that God does not breathe on the dead bones, even though He could have, since He is the source of all life; as Jesus demonstrated, He is the resurrection and the life (see John 11:25). Rather, He commands Ezekiel, the "son of man," to do it.

Likewise, our job is to prophesy—to be the conduit for the breath of God to flow into those who need supernatural life. It is similar to how the apostle Paul described our role in the world in Second Corinthians 5:20: "We are therefore Christ's ambassadors, as though God were making His appeal through us...." We are Jesus' hands and feet, as well as His mouth, on this earth, and He wants to breathe; He wants to exhale!

So then, when we prophesy, our words ride on the breath that is expelled from within us. Prophesying is simply exhaling in the Spirit, and the words that we speak, combined with the breath of the Spirit, bring life.

On one occasion, a grandfather approached me before a meeting that I was leading and asked if I would be willing to pray for his 2-year-old granddaughter who was in the ICU about 100 miles away. She was on a respirator and a feeding tube and had been given less than a 50-percent chance of living through the night. The grandfather added that she was also completely despondent.

After sharing the vision of the lion, I had the congregation stand up and breathe in the direction of the hospital. The next morning, the grandfather approached me before the service once again. This time he was overwhelmed with thankfulness because he had found out that, at the exact time that we had breathed, the little girl started breathing on her own, eating solid foods, and communicating as if nothing had been wrong. She was released from the hospital later that day, completely healed!

THE POWER OF OUR WORDS

We have the opportunity to bring life through the prophetic words that we speak. Solomon points out, "The tongue has the power of life and death..." (Prov. 18:21). In other words, our prophetic words have the ability to release the supernatural power of God.

In Genesis 1, when God created the universe and everything in it, He spoke and it came into existence. His word—His speech—had innate power to perform His will. It is as though each word has a specific mission to carry out God's plans and purposes.

In Isaiah 55:10-11, we learn:

As the rain and the snow come down from heaven, and do not return to it without watering the earth and making it bud and flourish, so that it yields seed for the sower and bread for the eater, so is My word that goes out from My mouth: It will not return to Me empty, but will accomplish what I desire and achieve the purpose for which I sent it.

So then, the words that we receive from the lion (Jesus) carry the power to perform the purpose for which He has breathed on us. His name(s) carry supernatural power; when we receive and release His Word, supernatural empowerment and breakthrough become possible. I believe that this principle explains why the gift of the word of knowledge is so effective in releasing physical healing, which is why I try to remember to utilize it wherever I go.

Recently, I was visiting the construction site for a Bible college in India. Upon finishing the tour of the grounds, I expressed to our guide that I felt like God wanted to heal a tumor of someone on the construction site.

He began to make inquiries and soon found out that the caretaker's wife was suffering from advanced breast cancer and had a huge tumor. Once I communicated to her the word of knowledge that I had received, I prayed for her. Immediately the tumor dissolved, and all of the pain subsided. Along with her husband, she began to cry tears of joy. She was completely healed by the Word and the Wind as I simply exhaled what I had inhaled.

When we release God's name (in this case, Healer), the Spirit will empower the words to accomplish His will. It just requires the faith to exhale what we receive from His breath—His presence.

In John 8:26, Jesus says, "...What I have heard from Him [the Father] I tell the world." In other words, Jesus breathed out—spoke what He had breathed in from the Father.

In John 3:32, John the Baptist confirms that Jesus testified (spoke) to only what He had seen and heard. He adds, in verse 34, "For the one whom God has sent speaks the words of God, for God gives the Spirit without limit."

In Matthew 8:23-27, in the middle of a life-threatening storm, Jesus speaks to the wind and the waves, and they become completely calm. The disciples are so amazed that they respond: "What kind of man is this? Even the winds and the waves obey Him!" (Matt. 8:27).

In the next chapter, Jesus speaks to a paralyzed man saying, "Get up, take your mat and go home" (Matt. 9:6), and the man is completely healed. Our words have power.

In Mark 7:31-35, some people bring a man who is deaf and mute to Jesus, begging Him to lay His hands on him to be healed. Instead, after putting His finger in the man's ears and putting His spit on the man's tongue, He speaks to the man, saying, "Be opened," and immediately his ears open, his tongue is loosed, and he begins to speak plainly—he is healed.

Isn't it interesting that He speaks to a man who could not hear? Why did He do it? Because He knew that there was power in the words He spoke, regardless of whether or not they could be heard in the natural. Jesus' words had power because He spoke them from the Father's presence—He spoke what He had inhaled.

Jesus spoke a word of forgiveness to a prostitute, and she was forgiven and set free (see John 8:3-11). He spoke to demons and they came out on command (see Matt. 8:16,32). The lame walked, the deaf heard, and the blind saw because He spoke the living, breathing Word of God wherever He went (see Matt. 4:23-24).

On one occasion, Jesus spoke to a fig tree, and it immediately withered (see Matt. 21:18-19). Obviously Jesus has the power of life and death in His tongue. When His disciples wondered at what had happened to the tree, Jesus instructed them that they could *speak* to a mountain and that it would be cast into the sea (see Matt. 21:21).

Our words can move mountains! Like Jesus, we are God's utterance— His speech—a communication of His creative will. Through the Holy Spirit's power, we can make a difference wherever we go.

Who Can Stop the Rain?

Bobby, a young man who lived with us for three years, was with my son, Chad, on a mission trip in Tijuana. They had scheduled a large outreach on Revolution Street, where there would be many who needed the Good News of Jesus.

Just after the team completed the set-up of the PA system, it started to rain. The forecast looked bleak, and many of the onlookers waited to see what the "gringos" would do in the face of the downpour.

Chad was discussing the fate of the outreach when Bobby grabbed the microphone and yelled out to those within earshot of the PA speakers, "Does anyone want to see a miracle? I'm going to speak to the clouds, and the rain is going to stop. Are you ready?" At that, the crowd cheered and jeered back, "Yes! Go ahead."

Bobby counted to three through the microphone and then spoke to the clouds, commanding them to part. On cue, the clouds began opening up to reveal a star-filled sky. The clouds continued rolling back until there was approximately a city-block-size circle of cloudless sky above the outreach. Amazingly, it was raining everywhere else.

Immediately many people came running toward the stage to get right with God, and many were saved, healed, and set free. Bobby changed the atmosphere because he realized that his words, empowered by the Holy Spirit, could make a difference.

"Let the Winds Blow Again"

It is not just the Word that brings about the will of God. The Wind—the Spirit of God—is equally important in accomplishing God's plans and purposes. Without breath, there is no life.

When God spoke, the universe and everything in it was created, including man (see Gen. 1:1-27). Adam did not become a living being, however, until God breathed on him (see Gen. 2:7). In Genesis 1:2, we are told that the Spirit of God was active in creation. We can assume, then, that the breath that God breathed into Adam was the Holy Spirit.

The Hebrew word for "Spirit/spirit" is *ruach (ruwach)*, and it can also mean "wind" or "breath." *Ruach* is translated in some passages as "wind" or "breath" (e.g. Ezek. 37:9).[4] The Hebrew word, *nashamach (neshamah)*, translated "breath" in Genesis 2:7, can also be used as a synonym for *ruach*—Spirit (e.g. Isa. 42:5).[5]

In the New Testament, the Greek word, *pneuma*, means "Spirit," "breath," or "wind."[6] In John 3:8, *pneuma* is translated as "wind" to describe the unseen dynamic of the Spirit.[7] Jesus breathed the Holy Spirit on His disciples in John 20:21-22, and they were anointed beyond their ability to carry out the impossible mission that they were sent to accomplish.

There is power in the breath of God. The apostle Paul points out that, when *the lawless one* is revealed, the Lord Jesus will overthrow him with the breath of His mouth (see 2 Thess. 2:8).

Jesus promised in Acts 1:8, "You will receive power when the Holy Spirit comes on you; and you will be My witnesses...." Later, when God breathed on the Church in the upper room on the day of Pentecost, the Church came to life (see Acts 2). A mighty wind came, and the disciples were empowered to demonstrate and release the Kingdom wherever they went. They preached, prophesied, healed the sick, and set people free because they had inhaled the empowering presence of God.

We not only need the wind (the Holy Spirit) to initiate us into ministry, but we also need ongoing encounters in which we inhale His breath. His breath not only creates and establishes life, but it also sustains and renews it.

During my first full-time ministry position as an associate pastor, many years ago, I suffered from burnout. I felt overworked and under-empowered to deal with the challenges and demands of pastoral ministry.

After two years, I decided to go back to seminary to work on a master's degree in Church Leadership Studies. Part of my purpose was to ascertain what I was lacking and to find some impetus to return to full-time career ministry and fulfill my destiny to impact the world.

I gained a lot of insight and wisdom during those years in pursuit of my degree, but in the end, I still felt disillusioned and discouraged about pursuing any full-time ministry positions. Instead, I went into sales and found that, as an evangelist, I was very good at influencing people to buy things from me.

I was soon making a lot of money, and after about five years, I had managed to attain the "yuppie" lifestyle of Southern California. The problem, however, was that I grew more and more depressed and cynical in my spirit. I was involved in Church ministry (as a home group leader), but my heart was not really in it; I was just going through the external motions. I felt spiritually dead inside.

Unfortunately, instead of turning to God for encouragement and strength, I turned toward material possessions, entertainment, and alcohol as a source of comfort. I was basically miserable, even though I masked it fairly well.

One Sunday, a prophet, Bob Jones, came to the church I was attending. I was scared to death because I thought he was going to call out all of my "sins" in front of the entire church. I knew that my heart had been far from God and that my lifestyle was not appropriate for a home group leader.

I felt some relief as he began to wind down his message without having called out anyone's sin. Then the unthinkable happened. He invited all of the leaders to come up on the stage because he wanted to lay hands on each one and prophesy over them.

I was terrified! My heart began to race while, on the outside, I was trying my best to play it cool. Meanwhile, my wife was so excited that she grabbed my hand and began rushing toward the stage. I tried to convince her that we could be last, thinking he might get tired and quit before we got up on the stage, but she was relentless.

Before I knew it, I was up on the stage. I began to shake and sweat. It was not the Holy Spirit. I was scared to death that Bob Jones was going to call down fire from God that would consume me on the spot. I imagined myself as the *Looney Tunes* cartoon character, Wile E. Coyote, who is always chasing after the Road Runner, when he gets blown up and all that is left is an outline of what used to be.

I reluctantly inched closer as my wife continued pulling me toward Judgment Day! It seemed to take years to get to the front of the line, and I spent the entire time repenting for anything that I could think of that might jeopardize my safety in some way.

Finally I was standing directly in front of Bob Jones. As I braced myself for the impending fire, he looked me in the eye and simply said, "Let the winds blow again." I must have looked confused because he reassured me: "That's right, son, let the winds blow again."

With that, I walked away, and after three steps, I fell on the stage in a heap of tears. I spent about 30 minutes crumpled up in a pool of tears and snot, feeling the winds of the Spirit breathing life back into me. I spent the next three months crying and laughing in His presence as the breath of God renewed the hopes and dreams that He had put in my heart.

Since that encounter many years ago (which the more-recent vision of the convertible and the lion only strengthened), I have learned to constantly position myself in the presence of God, inhaling His breath, as I allow His wind to blow in my face. When I begin to feel overwhelmed or powerless, I imagine the Lion standing in front of me, breathing the Holy Spirit's life into me.

As we feel empowered, we become more confident to release the Kingdom. In reality, we can only give away what we have received. The more we breathe in His presence, containing His powerful Word, the more we will be able to release the Kingdom to those around us. We will be able to do what Jesus did. We will be able to live a naturally supernatural life.

ENDNOTES

1. Gerhard Kittle, *Theological Dictionary of the New Testament,* vol. 4 (Grand Rapids, MI: Eerdmans, 1964), 69-136.

2. Ibid.

3. James Strong, "Greek Dictionary," *The New Strong's Expanded Exhaustive Concordance of the Bible* (Nashville, TN: Thomas Nelson, 2001), "charis" (#5485).

4. Kittle, *Theological Dictionary,* vol. 6, 332-451.

5. Ibid.

6. Ibid.

7. Strong, "Greek Dictionary," "pneuma" (#4151).

Chapter 8

COMPASSION IS SHOWN
IN ACTION

I'LL never forget the time when I was ministering to people in the prayer line after a Friday night service at Bethel Church. After praying for a few people, I noticed an elderly woman inching her way up to the prayer line with the aid of a walker. As I stood watching, she caught my eye and veered toward me with a determination indicating that she would not be denied.

Meeting her just beyond the front row, I noticed that she had a slipper on her right foot. When I inquired about the need for the slipper, the woman told me that she had an open-sore, cancerous tumor on the top of her foot. She went on to explain that she was scheduled to have her foot amputated the following Tuesday.

She then asked if I wanted to see it. My initial thought was, *Who in their right mind would want to see an open-sore, cancerous tumor?* Then I realized, "You don't tell grandma no." So, I said, "Sure, I would love to see your foot."

Her husband bent down and pulled off her slipper, revealing a lemon-sized tumor, open at the top and oozing pus. It was just about the grossest thing I have ever seen.

Just as I was doing all that I could not to vomit at the sight, I heard the Lord say, "I want you to reach down and touch it."

"What?"

"You heard Me," the Lord replied. "I want you to reach down and touch it."

Without even thinking, I responded, "No way!"

A third time the Lord told me to touch the woman's tumor, and He added, "I want you to touch it because I want to heal her like I healed the man with leprosy in Mark 1:40-42."

At this, I began looking around for a Bethel School of Supernatural Ministry student to come over and touch it so that the woman could be healed, but all of the students were busy praying for others. I was on my own.

All of a sudden, I was filled with an overwhelming sense of compassion for the woman that I knew was not my own. I could feel it rising up inside of me, to the point that I just had to do something to release God's power. So without even really thinking about it, I knelt down to pray for her foot.

I figured that she needed a major miracle, so instead of just putting the tip of my finger on her open sore, in order to fulfill the direction I had been given, I put my entire hand over the sore. It was gross, but I was so engulfed with a sense of wanting to help this woman that I put aside my repulsion.

As I prayed, she closed her eyes, tilted her head back, and began to sway and rock back and forth simultaneously, while holding on to her walker with both hands. Looking up, I knew that God was touching her in a powerful way, and after a few minutes, I asked what she was feeling.

She responded, "Oh, I feel so much peace. I have never felt like this before. This is amazing."

"That's great," I encouraged, "but what about your foot."

"I don't know about my foot, but I feel wonderful!" she exclaimed.

Over the years of praying for people for healing, I have learned to give thanks for whatever God is doing, no matter how seemingly insignificant it may seem at the time. (We will discuss this further in the next chapter.) With that in mind, I encouraged her to continue cultivating God's presence and went back to releasing the Kingdom on her tumor.

Soon she began swaying and rocking even more and would have fallen backward if her husband had not caught her and propped her back up. Once he got her upright, however, they both started swaying and rocking in exaggerated gyrations. At one point, I thought both of them were going to fall over backward and injure themselves.

After a few more minutes of watching her blissfully praising God without words, I asked once again how she felt. Once again, she responded: "I feel even better. I have never felt so much peace. This is amazing!"

Once again, I asked how her foot felt, thinking that it must have had some improvement since the last inquiry. Once again, to my chagrin, she indicated that she could not sense any difference in her foot but that the rest of her body felt great.

I prayed for a few more minutes, blessing the presence of God, who was riveting her body, and then encouraged her to go back to her hotel room and soak in the peace that she had been experiencing. Meanwhile, I was thinking, *This is great. I put my hand on the grossest thing imaginable, and nothing happened.*

Two weeks later, I received a letter from her. She thanked me for encouraging her to continue cultivating the peace that she had encountered that Friday night. She went on to write that she could not sleep all night long because the tumor on her foot kept becoming smaller and smaller.

Finally, when morning arrived, the tumor on her foot had completely dissolved. She ended the letter by informing me that she had called her doctor the first thing Monday morning to cancel the surgery to have her foot amputated! She was completely healed.

This all happened as a result of my response to the compassion that the Father had for this woman. It was not until I was supernaturally filled with His compassion that I had the impetus to reach down and touch her. This is the way that Jesus was motivated to reach out and touch people as well.

In Mark 1:40-42, we find an account of Jesus operating in the supernatural power of compassion. Mark describes the scene:

A man with leprosy came to Him [Jesus] *and begged Him on his knees, "If You are willing, You can make me clean."*

Filled with compassion, Jesus reached out His hand and touched the man. "I am willing," He said. "Be clean!" Immediately the leprosy left him and he was cured.

Compassion is a key ingredient in our ability to release the Kingdom. Compassion provides the motivation to reach out and touch those who need miraculous intervention. Thus, being filled with compassion is essential in living a naturally supernatural life.

Like Jesus, we have what people need, but it is compassion that releases what is inside of us—the supernatural presence of God to heal, save, and set people free.

Desperate People Do Desperate Things

Several years ago, I was visiting Huntington Beach, where my wife and I had planted and pastored a church for ten years. We were meeting with some of our former leaders for a dinner at a nice restaurant when a man came in looking very disheveled. He was bald, ashen white, and unusually thin for his frame, except that he looked about nine months pregnant.

He sat down right next to me, and I realized that it was Barry, a man I had led to Christ just before moving to Redding. The reason I did not recognize him was because he was in the fourth stage of pancreatic cancer.

Somehow he had found out that I was going to be at this particular restaurant, and without an invitation, in desperation, he came to the restaurant. He went on to explain that he had gone through all of the chemotherapy and radiation treatments without any improvement. The doctor was still giving him chemotherapy, but only for palliative purposes. The doctor had given him less than two weeks to live.

He continued to share that, as soon as he heard I was coming to visit, he knew that I could help him. To that end, he busted into our little party with no regard for protocol and without the thought that he might be interrupting our "closed" meeting. He was desperate, and desperate people do desperate things.

So right there in the restaurant, my wife and I, along with our former leaders, began to release the presence of God on him. Instantly he began to shake in response to God's power. Afterward he confessed that he had always mocked shaking manifestations, and with tears of joy in his eyes, he said that he felt heat and electricity going through his entire body.

The next night, we were meeting at the beach with some other friends and leaders from the church when I looked through the bonfire to see Barry coming toward us. Once again, he had found out where we were going to be and sought us out. He was desperate for more of God's healing presence. He needed a miracle and believed that we were the answer for his cure.

I got an email two weeks later saying that he was completely healed! He had a clean bill of health from the doctors, though they could not explain what had happened. Soon after, Barry sold everything he owned, and he is now somewhere in South America, preaching the Gospel and telling everyone about how God healed him and that He can heal them!

Most people do not have the wherewithal within to break into someone's space and request that their needs be met. Barry, like the leper in Mark 1, however, was desperate enough to risk any rejection, and as a result, his faith was rewarded.

In biblical times, leprosy was a deforming, flesh-eating disease that usually started with a small patch of white or pink discoloration of skin on the face. To the casual observer, it seemed insignificant and harmless. The discoloration, however, soon began to spread in all directions, eventually covering the entire body. Soon spongy tumors began appearing everywhere, and then the tissue between the bones in the hands and feet began to deteriorate, leaving tumorous stumps. In biblical times, there was no cure for leprosy, and it was thought to be very contagious, particularly through touch. Those who suffered from leprosy were sometimes quarantined, so that the disease would not spread.[1]

Leprosy was prevalent in the New Testament days, and common protocol declared it inappropriate for lepers to approach someone for any kind of help. Moreover, if you were a leper in those days, you were considered a social outcast. You were untouchable. The leper in Mark 1 went against all cultural mores to gain access to Jesus.

According to the Old Testament Mosaic Law, if you touched a leper, you were considered spiritually unclean. Lepers, therefore, were required by law to warn anyone who came within a certain distance that they had the disease. They were to yell, "Unclean. Unclean." As a result, lepers were also spiritual outcasts.

So here is this grotesquely deformed, tumor-ridden leper in Mark 1, who is considered unclean, coming to Jesus, begging on his knees. In his desperation, instead of yelling out "unclean," he asks Jesus to touch him. This man had obviously heard about what Jesus could do, and he knew that He had the cure.

The only thing that was holding back the cure, in the mind of the leper, was whether or not Jesus was willing to take a risk and touch him. I'm sure everyone at the scene was wondering how Jesus would respond. Like I did when the woman came to me with the cancerous tumor, I'm sure I would have been looking around for one of the disciples to come and touch him.

Jesus, on the other hand, was instantly "filled with compassion" (Mark 1:41). He received something that he did not have before that moment, and He reached out and touched the man. Compassion became the motivating force for the release of the Kingdom for this man who had no other hope of a cure.

DO YOU HAVE THE GUTS?

Some Bible translations, like the English Standard Version, use the word *pity,* in verse 41, to describe Jesus' motivation. *Pity,* however, best corresponds with the Greek word *oikteiro* (verb), which means "filled with sorrow," or "a feeling of distress through the ills of others. It is a characteristic that Paul is looking for in the Philippians (see Phil. 2:1)."[2] Pity is what you might feel when seeing a homeless person on the street—you feel sorry for him. Pity means feeling bad for someone when you find out that they have cancer. Pity says, "Wow, what a shame; that's a really bad break; bummer for you." Pity causes you to feel bad for people, but it does not motivate you to help them. Jesus was not filled with pity.

Jesus was not filled with sympathy either. The Greek word *sumpatheo* (generally translated "sympathy") means, " 'I feel bad with you. I understand your pain. I can identify with you. I suffer with you.' The writer to the Hebrews in 10:34 uses this word as he encourages those who have had sympathy for those in prison."[3] Now certainly, it is admirable to identify with the suffering of those who have been put in prison as a result of being persecuted for the Gospel, but sympathy does not get the person out of prison! Several years ago, I was in a hotel room when I accidentally cut the two toes on my left foot down to the bone. I had slipped off of a step leading to the bed and caught my toes on a protruding metal light cover that was built into the step. It had apparently been bent out by a maid aggressively cleaning with the vacuum cleaner.

Lying on the floor, I yelled to my wife that I had just cut my toes and that she should turn the light on. Knowing what a prankster I can be at times, she playfully told me to knock off my joking and come to bed. Finally I convinced her to turn on the light, and then I let go of my toes. Blood squirted across the ceiling, and she screamed loud enough to raise the dead!

When I arrived at the Emergency Room by ambulance, they laid me face down on a gurney and bent my leg up at a 90-degree angle at the knee so that the doctor could attempt to reconnect my toes to my foot.

I have never experienced such pain in my life. Each time that the doctor shot the lidocaine into my toes, it felt like white-hot lightning. Even worse, because of the severe bleeding, the numbing agent flowed right out with the blood. Just when the doctor would get the stitching hook into my toe, I would regain all sensitivity.

I had been bear-hugging the gurney for about a half an hour when the doctor decided to take a break, leaving me soaked in sweat. I guess all of my screaming and hyperventilating (like a woman in extreme labor) was just too much for him to handle.

Just then, without an invitation, a woman who had been in the next compartment opened the drapes and came barging into my space. She had apparently overheard my nightmarish ordeal and decided to come over and comfort me.

The woman began to tell me about a time when she had cut her finger to the bone while preparing food. She went into all of the gory details, highlighting all of the painful memories. She was doing her best to comfort me with sympathy—she could relate to my pain because she had gone through the same thing.

After a few minutes, I looked up at her, still hyperventilating and soaked in sweat, and said, "You are not helping me right now. I don't care about your finger; I need a new toe! Please leave!" At that moment, I did not need sympathy; I needed compassion.

In Mark 1:41, the Greek verb used here for "filled with compassion" is *splagchnizomai. Splagchnizomai* ("compassion," in verb form) means seeing the pain (pity), feeling and understanding the pain (sympathy), and more importantly, being compelled to do something practical *for* the pain.[4] Isn't it interesting that the Greek word used here is a verb, an *action* word? Compassion involves the willingness to act when we see someone in need, whatever that need may be. Jesus was filled with compassion.

Compassion is much more than a superficial, "Hope you get well" platitude or a consoling, "I understand." No, compassion moves us to action. It is birthed out of an intense passion and desire to help in a practical way. Compassion causes us to rise up and make a difference. Thankfully, the doctor who reattached my toes demonstrated compassion!

Interestingly, the Greek word used to describe Judas spilling his "bowels" (*splagchnon*) on the rocks after he flung himself from a cliff (see Acts 1:18) is the noun counterpart for the verb *splagchnizomai*.[5] Thus, *splagchnizomai* (having compassion) represents the deepest part of our being; it is something that explodes from deep within us.

Jesus was filled with compassion, which caused something inside of Him to explode, and that motivated Him to reach out and touch this ugly, unclean, leprous man. From deep inside His guts—the deepest part of His being—He said, "I am willing...." In other words, He said, "I am ready to do something about this"—that is compassion.

In Matthew 14:14, Jesus saw a crowd of people who had followed Him out to a deserted place, and "...He had compassion on them and healed their sick." It was the compassion that motivated Him to do something practical to meet the needs represented. Not only did He heal their sick, but He also provided a meal that fed everyone (see Matt. 14:15-21).

In First John 3:17-18, it says, "If anyone has material possessions and sees his brother in need but has no pity on him, how can the love of God be in him?" Here "pity" is not the Greek word *oikteiro*. Rather, it is the Greek word *splagchnon*—compassion, the same word sometimes translated "bowels." In fact, the KJV translates the word in this passage as "bowels of compassion." John was not instructing his readers to "feel bad" (have pity) for those they saw with need, but rather, to do something about what they saw. *Compassion* is a demonstration that the love of God is in us.

I love the parable about the Good Samaritan in Luke 10. Jesus used this story to communicate what it looks like to love God practically. He says:

"A man was going down from Jerusalem to Jericho, when he fell into the hands of robbers. They stripped him of his clothes, beat him and went away, leaving him half dead. A priest happened to be going down

the same road, and when he saw the man, he passed by on the other side. So too, a Levite, when he came to the place and saw him, passed by on the other side. But a Samaritan, as he traveled, came where the man was; and when he saw him, he took pity on him. He went to him and bandaged his wounds, pouring on oil and wine. Then he put the man on his own donkey, took him to an inn and took care of him. The next day he took out two silver coins and gave them to the innkeeper. 'Look after him,' he said, 'and when I return, I will reimburse you for any extra expense you may have.'

"Which of these three do you think was a neighbor to the man who fell into the hands of robbers?"

The expert in the law replied, "The one who had mercy on him."

Jesus told him, "Go and do likewise" (Luke 10:30-37).

Once again, the Samaritan did not have "pity" on the man, as it is translated in the NIV. He had *splagchnizomai* (compassion) for him, which prompted him to do something to help the man. Jesus is pointing out that true love for God manifests in helping people in practical ways. In other words, compassion is shown in action.

TOUCHING TRANSFORMATION

After being a Christian for about two years, I had a vision that inspired me to pursue a full-time career in pastoral, public ministry. In the vision, I found myself on a cold, damp, dirty street at night, surrounded by drunk homeless people who were disheveled and dirty-looking.

Some were sleeping on benches with newspapers covering them to provide some insulation from the cold, damp night; others were so drunk and tired that they just lay in the garbage-filled gutters or on the filthy sidewalk. Some were huddled together in a side alley in misery. It was a scene of absolute depression and utter hopelessness.

As I was standing in the middle of all of this, a man approached me who seemed to be worse off than the rest. He looked like he had not had a bath in *forever*. His hair was matted in every direction and hung in clumps over his bloodshot eyes.

Some of his front teeth were missing, and the ones that were left were yellow and rotting. I could smell his foul breath as he wheezed through swollen, cracked lips. His scraggly beard looked as though it contained fragments of debris from every place he had ever been over the previous six months. His six-foot-two frame could have easily carried 225 pounds, but he could not have weighed more than 160.

His clothing was ragged and smelled worse than he did. Nothing in his wardrobe matched, and it was obvious that he did not care. He looked even more depressed and hopeless than the environment around him.

As he stood in front of me, pleading with his eyes for me to do something to help him, my first instinct was to run! He looked scary, and it took all of my willpower to stay. Then, I found myself thinking, *What do you want from me? This is your fault. Get a job!*

Then the Lord spoke to me in the vision and said, "Kevin, reach out and touch him."

I responded, "Are You kidding?" I know that seems like a stupid response, but I'm just relating the facts.

Patiently the Lord repeated, "Kevin, would you please reach out and touch him?" Immediately, I saw him through eyes of compassion, and I reached out and touched him.

As soon as I laid my hand on him, he started transforming before my eyes. His hair was suddenly short, cut in a business style, and he became clean-shaven. His bloodshot eyes converted to a clear, vibrant blue that was full of life. His teeth suddenly turned bright white, and the caverns of missing teeth were replaced.

He was now completely clean and finely groomed. He was dressed in an expensive suit with an exquisitely matching tie. Even his Italian shoes put the final touch on his new GQ look.

Amazingly, the transformation did not stop with him. As it had started from his head and progressed to his shoes, it continued spreading onto the sidewalk. Everything began to transform around us. The litter-filled street was now sparkling clean.

The dampness of the darkness was gone, turned instead into a sunny day. No one was sleeping in the gutters, on benches, or in alleyways, hungover in hopelessness. In fact, everyone was now dressed in business suits and smiling at each other as they passed by. The entire city was being transformed before my eyes.

Then, the Lord spoke to me once again: "Kevin, if you are willing to reach out and touch those who seem unclean, despicable, and hopeless, I will heal them and transform them." And then He showed me that I had been seeing people from the inside out. "You see, Kevin," the Lord went on, "there are many who are lepers on the inside and who need to be touched."

Since then, I have tried on purpose to reach out and touch people in Jesus' name and to give them what they need. I find that, when I am filled with supernatural compassion, I can release His supernatural Kingdom to those whom God puts in my path.

REVIVAL CLOTHES

Compassion is not a natural human trait. It comes from God. Even Jesus was "filled with compassion" in Mark 1:41. Jesus did not walk around with innate compassion; in His humanity, He had to be filled, and so do we. He needed an impartation of what He did not possess on His own. Likewise, we must receive an impartation of the Father's compassion if we want to live naturally supernatural lives.

In Colossians 3:12, we are challenged with this command: "Therefore, as God's chosen people, holy and dearly loved, clothe yourselves with compassion...." The Father has provided a garment of compassion for us, but we must put it on; we must wear what is available to us in order to be equipped for the demands that await us.

It's kind of like Clark Kent going into the phone booth to put on his Superman suit. Without the suit, Clark is just an ordinary guy with no power to help anyone. Once he puts the suit on, however, he is empowered to rescue and intervene for those in need.

So it is for the believer. Without the clothing of compassion, nothing rises up in us to destroy the works of the devil or to help and intervene for those in need. If we want to be revivalists who make history and change the world—if we want to live naturally supernatural lives—we must be clothed in compassion. Only then will we make a difference in the sphere of influence where God has placed us to bring transformation.

JESUS HEALED HIM; JESUS SAVED HIM

Recently I heard a testimony from one of our graduates of the Bethel School of Supernatural Ministry. She was on her way to church one Sunday morning when she came upon an accident. She instantly knew that she was supposed to stop; she felt compelled to try to help in some way.

After parking on the side of the freeway, she noticed a man lying on a gurney. Oddly, no one was around him, so she went over to see if he might need prayer. As soon as he saw her, he exclaimed, "You're the angel. You're the angel."

"No, I'm not, but I *am* a Christian," she responded.

Once again, looking up at her, he countered, "No, you're the angel that I saw just before the accident!"

She countered once again, "Sir, I'm really not an angel, but could I pray for you?"

He agreed, telling her that, as a result of the accident, he could not feel his legs; he was paralyzed from the waist down.

Without hesitation, she began to release the Kingdom over him, and immediately he threw his legs over the side of the gurney and stood up. He began running around her and the gurney, shouting out that he was completely healed. She then led him into a relationship with Jesus on the spot!

Just then, a highway patrolman came over to where the two were rejoicing and demanded to know what was happening. He was very upset because he had left the man in a paralyzed condition just a few minutes earlier.

The student looked at the officer and simply said, "Well, Jesus just healed him, and Jesus just saved him."

The officer shot back, "That's ridiculous!" Turning toward the man, he asked him what had happened to enable him to walk. He said, "Like she said, officer, Jesus just healed me, and Jesus just saved me!"

Now perturbed, the patrolman said, "I can't write that on the report."

The student countered, "Then we can't sign it."

Now resigned, the patrolman began to write, mouthing the words as he wrote: "Jesus healed him, and Jesus saved him."

When we are filled with compassion, as Jesus was in Mark 1, we will be more motivated to stop, and then we will find that we really do have the ability to meet the needs of those we reach out to. It is a partnership to release the Kingdom—doing God's will on earth as it is in Heaven.

God's part, then, is to provide the supernatural motivation, and our part is to have the willingness to reach out. It was only after Jesus was filled with compassion that He followed with the statement, "I am willing" (Mark 1:41).

In His willingness to take risk, Jesus touched the man. As a result, the man was immediately cured (see Mark 1:42). When we are willing to take risk, touching those around us who have intimidating needs, we release supernatural possibilities. When we, motivated by compassion, touch people, supernatural power is activated.

I have found that, when I am clothed with compassion on a daily basis, I cannot help but reach out to help those who are desperate. The need to act explodes out of the deepest part of my being. This is the way to unlock Heaven. This is the way to live a naturally supernatural life.

I would encourage you to take time each morning, before you leave your home for the day's activities, to get into God's presence, to go to the compassion closet, and to put on His supernatural compassion suit.

And then, being clothed in compassion, when you see the lepers, you will have something to give them. You will be able to truly provide a cure, whether it is healing, forgiveness, an encouraging prophetic word, an act of kindness or service, wisdom, emotional freedom, or spiritual renewal.

You have been called to be a revivalist—a world changer—a history-maker. You have been called to bring Heaven to earth as Christ's ambassador. Two questions remain: are you clothed, and are you willing?

ENDNOTES

1. "Leper; Leprosy," *The International Standard Bible Encyclopedia,* http://www.studylight.org/enc/isb/view.cgi?number=T5483 (accessed Dec. 30, 2008).

2. W.E. Vine, *Vine's Expository Dictionary of New Testament Words* (McLean, VA: MacDonald Publishing Company, n.d.), 744.

3. Vine, *Vine's Expository Dictionary,* 220.

4. Gerhard Kittle, *Theological Dictionary of the New Testament,* vol. 7 (Grand Rapids, MI: Eerdmans, 1964), 548-559.

5. Vine, *Vine's Expository Dictionary,* 220.

Chapter 9

PREPARING FOR BREAKTHROUGH

I N 2002, my wife and I had been in public, full-time ministry for about 20 years. We had planted an amazing church in Huntington Beach, California, that we pastored for over ten years. Our church had seen hundreds of people come into God's Kingdom as a result of our many outreach activities. We were at a place, however, where we knew that there had to be more for our lives as we pursued God, and more through our lives as we sought to make a difference in the world to expand God's Kingdom here on the earth.

We were looking into joining a large pastoral staff at a church in Oregon, where we could develop and deploy church-planting teams throughout the Pacific Northwest. As we were sharing our plans to visit the church with some pastor friends of ours, they suggested that we stop on the way at a church called Bethel, in Redding, California. There they said we could get refreshed and revitalized. Prior to this conversation, we had never heard of Bethel Church or of Bill Johnson, but after doing an Internet search, we decided to visit during a Friday night service.

At the end of the service, Theresa exclaimed that Bethel was the place where God was calling us to fulfill our destiny. My immediate response was,

"No way! It was a great meeting, but Redding is basically a truck stop. Furthermore, we don't know anyone here, and what would we do for employment?" The list of negatives continued through the evening.

The next morning, I was reading some select passages from a daily Bible reading program that I had been doing for several months. One of the passages just happened to be Genesis 28. As I read, I was amazed at how I had been set up by God.

In the chapter, Jacob has deceived his brother Esau out of his inheritance, and as a result, he has to flee to his uncle Laban's house to find asylum from Esau's anger. Along the way, he camps at a place called Luz. That night he has a dream in which the Lord tells him that his descendants are going to be as numerous as the grains of sand on the seashore and that they will come from the north, south, east, and west. The Lord tells Jacob that he is going to come back to this land in which he has had the dream. When he wakes up, he proclaims, "This is none other than Bethel" (see Gen. 28:16-19).

Imagine that—God can even speak to us through a directed reading program! I knew that God had spoken to me out of the proverbial burning bush, but I still wanted to check out the opportunity in Oregon. After experiencing one service at the church in Oregon, I knew that Bethel was the place for us. Sheepishly, I confessed my earlier encounter with Genesis 28, to which Theresa replied with an enthusiastic, "I told you so!"

We had no job offer and knew no one in the city, but we were hungry for more of God, and we knew that Bethel was a place where our hunger could be satisfied. Full of excitement and anticipation, we sped back to Huntington Beach the next morning and put our house on the market that evening. Amazingly, it sold in just 45 minutes for the full asking price! The real estate agent did not even have time to put the sign up.

That next Sunday, we resigned from the church, and in 40 days, we had moved and bought a house in Redding, California, even though most of our friends thought we were crazy. We were hungry for revival, and we were ready to pay any price to get it.

Moreover, even though I have two theological degrees (and Theresa has her bachelor's degree in Psychology with a Biblical Studies minor) and many years of pastoral ministry experience, we decided that the way to get more impartation, empowerment, and activation was to attend Bethel School of Supernatural Ministry. We enrolled our entire family and spent a year getting retooled for a revival lifestyle in which the supernatural became normal.

We used up our entire savings and profit from our house in that year, but it was one of the best years of our lives. We would come home at night and discuss all of the paradigm shifts we were making related to our new-found understanding of the Kingdom being released in and through our lives. More importantly, we began to see the miraculous flowing through us on a regular basis as we stepped out to take risks.

Hunger Attracts Heaven

Hunger also releases the favor of God as Heaven comes, which makes a pathway into a seeker's destiny. After that first year in Redding, we were asked to join the Bethel pastoral staff, and it has been amazing ever since. I have traveled all over the world, releasing a Kingdom revival culture. Along the way, I have seen hundreds of people healed, saved, and set free as the goodness and kindness of God are demonstrated in signs and wonders, miracles, healing, prophetic words, and supernatural evangelism.

I truly believe that our hunger for God and His Kingdom paved a way for the opportunities that my family and I enjoy today, as well as the regular breakthroughs that we are seeing in the miraculous. Our sustained hunger is continuing to unlock Heaven all around us.

HUNGER PREPARES THE WAY FOR BREAKTHROUGH

Hunger may be the most significant key to releasing the Kingdom in and through our lives. In Hebrews 11:6, we are promised that "...He rewards those who earnestly seek Him."

One of the nuanced meanings of the phrase "earnestly seek" in the Greek is to "crave."[1] Accordingly, when we crave His presence and the resources of His Kingdom, He rewards us with His presence and power. Therefore, if we desire greater breakthrough in the miraculous, we must continually stay hungry. Hunger unlocks the resources of Heaven and releases them on earth.

In Psalm 34:10, David testifies that "...those who seek the Lord lack no good thing," and in Psalm 107:9, he further promises that "He [God] satisfies the thirsty and fills the hungry with good things." This was not only David's personal experience with God, but it is also a prophetic promise about the Messiah coming to bring the Good News (the good things) of the Kingdom.

In Luke 1:53, Mary sings these prophetic words, written by David, in response to the angel's announcement that she has been chosen to be the bearer of the Messiah: "He has filled the hungry with good things...." Could it be that Mary was chosen to bring forth the Messiah because of her hunger for God's Kingdom to come?

Could it be that the hunger of a few simple people, like Simeon, Anna, and Mary, attracted Heaven, bringing it to earth? Could it be that "at just the right time" (Rom. 5:6) is determined by our hunger for God and His Kingdom? There was a 400-year season of silence prior to Jesus' coming. Could it be that hunger broke the silence and released the Good News?

For example, Mary unlocked Heaven at the wedding at Cana when she asked Jesus to provide wine for the wedding party (see John 2:1-11). Mary's hunger was relentless, even though Jesus chided, "Why do you involve Me? My time has not yet come." Her hunger was demonstrated by a "deaf ear" to Jesus' response and expressed in her command to the servants when she said, "Do what He says." Water was turned into wine that day, and Jesus exposed Himself as the promised Messiah *before* the time that God had planned in Heaven because of Mary's hunger for God's intervention in a crisis.

In First Corinthians 14:1, the apostle Paul encourages us to "...eagerly desire spiritual gifts...." To that end, David testifies in Psalm 21:2, "You have granted him the desire of his heart...." When we crave God's presence, we are in turn rewarded with all of the good things of His Kingdom.

It is the Father's heart to give us every perfect gift (see James 1:17), whether it is provision, encouragement, comfort, wisdom, signs and wonders, miracles, or healing. It is our hunger that attracts the good things that we want from God and His Kingdom.

Many times, at the end of a meeting, someone will approach me who desperately needs a miracle. Even though I am completely exhausted, I will stop to pray for them because of their hunger. In fact, the more hunger I sense, the longer I will contend with them for a breakthrough miracle. I believe God responds to us in a similar fashion. When He senses our hunger, He shows up.

Conversely, when I sense that someone is not hungry for me to pray for them, but has sort of a nonchalant attitude, I am not normally very motivated to sacrifice in contending for breakthrough with them—mostly because I have not seen very much happen where there is no hunger.

In Matthew 15:29-38, Jesus has been ministering to a multitude of people for an extended period of time. The disciples suggest that He send them away because they are hungry and there is not enough food to go around. Instead of sending them away, however, Jesus feeds them. Jesus did not turn away from hungry people when He walked the earth, and He does not turn away from those who hunger for His Kingdom now. When fulfilling our desires, God is motivated by our hunger and thirst.

In John 6:35, Jesus proclaimed, "I am the bread of life. He who comes to Me will never go hungry, and he who believes in Me will never be thirsty." Notice, He does not say that we will not get hungry again, but rather, that we will not continue to be hungry. In other words, our hunger and thirst will be satisfied, and we will never experience lack.

Similarly, in Matthew 5:6, Jesus promises, "Blessed are those who hunger and thirst for righteousness, for they will be filled." Over and over, we find examples of hunger for God's Kingdom leading to resources being filled and satisfied.

Blind Bartimaeus was hungry for God; he was desperate for Jesus to heal him. As Jesus passed by, he began to shout out, "Son of David, have mercy on me" (Mark 10:48). The crowd told him to be quiet, but he just got louder. Bartimaeus wanted his healing, and his hunger attracted Heaven. When Jesus stopped, He healed him, and Bartimaeus was satisfied.

In Mark 5:25-34, we read about a woman who had a bleeding condition for 12 years. She was so hungry for healing that she pressed through the crowd to touch Jesus. Her hunger attracted Heaven, and she was healed.

In Luke 5:17-26, the friends of a paralytic somehow hoisted him up onto the roof of the house where Jesus was ministering, and then they lowered him through an opening that they made in the roof. Jesus saw their faith, represented in their hunger for a miracle, and He healed the man.

The Syrophoenician woman in Mark 7:24-30 was hungry for the healing of her daughter. Her desperate desire was revealed by her response when Jesus denied her request. She said, "Even the dogs get the leftovers" (my paraphrase). Her hunger attracted Heaven, and her daughter was healed.

In the parable of the persistent widow, Jesus depicts how hunger can persuade even the most indifferent of judges to grant a request (see Luke 18:1-8). The widow's hunger, expressed in her persistent petitioning of the judge, brought about the breakthrough that she needed. How much more will God reward our persistence and give us the desires of our hearts when we pursue Him for the things that we need!

So many times I have prayed for someone without results on the first attempt. I could have easily quit, but because I was desperate to see the Kingdom released to help the person, I persisted on to see a breakthrough miracle. Sometimes, I have prayed four or five times before breakthrough for healing came.

Through the years, I have learned that, even when I do not see immediate breakthrough, I can know that hunger has attracted Heaven and will eventually result in good things. Hunger prepares the way for breakthrough. Hunger unlocks Heaven.

TESTIMONIES CREATE HUNGER

While writing this chapter, I was in Ecuador working with a network of churches to equip, empower, and activate them in a supernatural lifestyle. While in the city of Cuenca, I was invited to speak on a radio station with over 10,000 listeners during a particular time slot. I began to speak about living a naturally supernatural life—sharing testimonies of how signs and wonders, miracles, healing, and the prophetic should be a natural part of the believer's life.

Ten minutes into the program, the phone lines began to light up as listeners heard about the hope of healing coming through the release of God's supernatural Kingdom. In desperation, they called, wanting to get healed.

The staff became frantic, trying to keep up with the volume of calls, and informed me that they had never received so many calls during a show.

The first woman who called said that she had pain in her kidneys and feet. I could sense her desperation and immediately began to release the Kingdom of God to her over the airwaves. She expressed that she felt a fiery heat throughout her body and could feel healing coming into her feet and kidneys.

Without really thinking, I asked through the translator, "What about your head? Do you have a headache?"

"*Si*," she responded in Spanish.

I continued, "Do you have pain in your neck and your shoulders?"

"*Si!*" she exclaimed.

"How about your lower back?"

"*Si!*"

"What about your knee?"

"*Si!* How do you know all of that?" she inquired.

I explained that God showed me her pain because He wanted to heal every part of her.

I released the fire of God to her, and in about 30 seconds, she was completely healed from head to toe. She testified that all of the pain had left her body and that she was now standing, which was miraculous in itself because prior to the phone call she had been paralyzed!

Caller after caller shared their desperation for healing, and time after time, God's power was released to make them well. The radio station had never had so many calls, and a one-hour show turned into two! We could have kept going all day long. The phone lines were still lit up as we walked out the door to our next appointment!

On the way out, however, we were informed that a woman had called saying that she was driving down to the station. She needed a miracle, and she had asked if we could please wait for a few minutes. When she arrived, the fire of God immediately fell over her entire body, and she was healed of several debilitating ailments, including fibromyalgia and a herniated disk.

Afterward, she told us that she had awakened that morning and said to herself, *What's the use? This is going to be another day of pain and hopelessness.* She went on to say that she had decided not to go to work because she had felt so miserable. She decided to turn on the radio, however, and heard me sharing testimonies of how God can help us supernaturally.

After hearing a few testimonies of people being healed, she felt compelled to call the station, but she could not get her call through until I was already off the air. Instead of giving up, however, she was fueled on by her desperate hunger, caused by the testimonies, and she drove to the radio station, where she received her miracle breakthrough. Her hunger prepared the way for breakthrough and unlocked Heaven for her.

Cultivating a Lifestyle of Hunger

When I think of people who have demonstrated spiritual hunger, resulting in supernatural breakthrough, I am reminded of the 120 in the upper room on the day of Pentecost. For ten days they sought God in prayer, anticipating the coming of the Holy Spirit upon the Church, and then suddenly, their hunger attracted Heaven, and all of them were filled with the Spirit and power (see Acts 1:12-15; 2:1-4,43).

I have often wondered what happened to the more than 500 who had seen Jesus resurrected (see 1 Cor. 15:6) but who were not in the upper room on that epic day on which Heaven was unlocked? Could it be that they started out with the 120 but lost desire once the wait for the Spirit's coming exceeded the "few days" that Jesus had promised before He ascended to Heaven (see Acts 1:5)?

Could it be that they had no hunger to pursue the Kingdom once they encountered the risen Lord and that they subsequently missed out on revival? I wonder how many have had an encounter with Jesus at some point in their life, only to stop seeking and end up missing out on the wonders and goodness that He had in store for them if they would have continued to daily encounter His presence.

For several years, we had a family Thanksgiving tradition in which my son and I, along with all of the other guys who were invited to our day of feasting, would weigh in at the beginning of the day. Our goal was to see who could eat the most in one day. All day long, we would devour everything in sight. We always started with all of the wonderful appetizers that my wife and others had prepared for us to enjoy while watching football.

Then there was the meal itself: the turkey, mashed potatoes, sweet potatoes, my wife's special dressing, and all of the rest of the trimmings that one would expect for a Thanksgiving feast. After dinner, we would polish off as much pie as we could push into our bloated bellies.

Finally, at the appointed time, we would line up to weigh in one last time to celebrate our results. I held the record of 14 pounds! But eventually I had to ban the tradition because I found out that I could no longer drop the weight like I had in previous years.

Pursuing Kingdom breakthrough is founded upon our ability to stay spiritually hungry. Importantly, spiritual hunger is a developed discipline that must be cultivated on a regular basis. Much like we encouraged physical hunger during our family's traditional Thanksgiving feast, we have tried to encourage spiritual hunger as a family over the years. To that end, I believe that our commitment to cultivating spiritual hunger has prepared us for the supernatural breakthroughs that we are currently experiencing in our lives and ministry.

My son, Chad, is a prime example of someone who has cultivated hunger for God and His Kingdom. Once he finally committed his life to Christ, just before his senior year in high school, he developed an insatiable appetite for God's presence.

I remember, one day, I walked into his room as he and two friends were laid out on the floor worshiping God. I asked him to mow the lawn because it was one of his weekly responsibilities. He looked at me with forlorn eyes and said, "Dad, please let me just worship for one more hour."

I was so used to hearing other excuses like, "I'm too tired," "I'll do it tomorrow," or "It doesn't need to be mowed this week—the lawn looks fine," that I did not even really hear what he had said. So, on automatic pilot, I responded, "Chad, I need you to do it now."

He was relentless, however, and pushed the point, pleading, "Dad, I want to take care of my responsibilities, but I have never experienced God's love like I am right now."

It finally registered with me that he was communicating hunger. At that, I quickly encouraged him to take as long as he wanted, but only under the condition that he would agree to take the presence of God with him to mow the lawn before it got dark in a few hours!

A few years later, my wife and I became overseers at the Bethel School of Supernatural Ministry. My son was attending the school, and during his second year, we were overseers of his class. A few months into the school year, I began to notice that he would be missing from class for prolonged periods of time.

Finally one day I decided to find out why he was cutting class, so I followed him. Without any wasted time, he made his way into the first-year room, where a guest speaker was giving an impartation. And then, as if he was a first-year student, he got into the line to get whatever the guest was releasing.

Chad has been like that ever since he completely gave his life to Christ at age 16. He is just hungry. His appetite for God and His Kingdom is insatiable. He is content, but never satisfied—he is always hungry for more. As a result, he routinely releases Heaven wherever he goes—his hunger has attracted Heaven, which is demonstrated in signs and wonders, miracles, healing, the prophetic, and supernatural evangelism.

My daughter, Alexa, is the same way. I will never forget a time when she was around 10 years old. We had been at Bethel Church for about a year. It was bedtime, we had said our "goodnights," and the lights were out. About 20 minutes later, as I was walking down the hallway, I heard music coming from her room. I opened the door and began lecturing her on the rules of bedtime. Immediately she interrupted, pleading, "But Dad, this is my soaking time!"

Instantly, I rebuked myself for thinking that she was just unwilling to go to bed. She was hungry, and she had to eat! My daughter, who is now 16, has cultivated a lifestyle of hunger for God's presence, and as a result, she lives a naturally supernatural life.

In Psalm 42:1-2, David says this of his desire for God: "As the deer pants for streams of water, so my soul pants for You, O God. My soul thirsts for God, for the living God...." In Psalm 143:6, he adds, "...My soul thirsts for You like a parched land." This is the way that I try to live my life every day—

hungering and thirsting for God and His Kingdom, which is a primary key to living a naturally supernatural life.

Cultivating our spiritual hunger prepares the way for God's Kingdom to come into our lives. Like my response to a Thanksgiving feast, our spiritual hunger prepares the way for breakthrough.

WE CAN HAVE AS MUCH AS WE WANT

I love going to all-you-can-eat buffets. There is just something about having access to an endless array of delectable appetizers, entrees, supplementary sides, and desserts that drives me toward the verge of gluttony. On one occasion, when I was much younger, I went through the line so many times that I was on a first-name basis with the servers!

Going to buffets is frustrating these days because I tend to get full before I can sample everything available; I can only eat a small percentage of what I could devour when I was younger, when I had a much higher metabolism. It is disappointing to not have the capacity to take in all that I want!

Age and metabolism, however, do not affect God's buffet—we can have as much of Him as we want! We can have as much of the Kingdom as we want. We can have as much breakthrough as we want! The question is, "How much can we eat?" The answer to that question will determine the amount of breakthrough we will experience in the Kingdom; Heaven will open up commensurate to our hunger.

We can only give away what we have received. And the amount that we receive from God is contingent upon our hunger level. I have found that, the hungrier I am, the more breakthroughs I experience.

I would like to suggest that we could grow in our hunger for God and the things of His Kingdom. The more regularly I eat, the greater capacity I have for more. It is that way in the natural, and it is the same in the supernatural.

I once fasted with some of the leaders of our church in Huntington Beach for seven days with just water. Afterward, we went to a steak and seafood restaurant and ordered practically everything on the menu. We each took about four bites and could not eat any more. It took me two more days to eat that one meal because my stomach had shrunk so small.

It is the same way in the spiritual realm. The more we consume the presence of God, the greater our capacity becomes. When we starve ourselves from His presence, our capacity to contain His presence diminishes.

We can have as much of God and His Kingdom as we desire, but the determining factor is our level of hunger and our capacity to consume. In order for that increase to happen, we must put ourselves in places where we are stretched to get more.

WHO WANTS MORE?

In Psalm 34:8, David invites us to "taste and see that the Lord is good...." This invitation is followed by a promise: "...Blessed is the man who takes refuge in Him." In other words, when you take just one bite, you will taste His goodness, and you will want more. You will take refuge, you will jump in all the way, and you will be happy that you did!

It is kind of like the scene in the movie *Patch Adams* where Patch, a medical school student, prepares a pool of spaghetti for one of his patients to swim in. She so liked spaghetti that she wanted to take *refuge* in it—that is what hunger will do for you.

It is the same in the Kingdom. Once you get even a little taste of the heavenly realm and find that it is good, you will become hungry for more.

It is like going to the all-you-can-eat buffet and taking a small portion of something that you have never eaten before. Once you taste it and like it, you become hungry for more.

When the woman at the well met Jesus and found out that He had water that could fulfill her, she responded, "Give me this water..." (John 4:15). Her thirst for the supernatural water that Jesus spoke of broke open the floodgates of Heaven for her life.

In Acts 9, we find an account of a man who has a taste of Heaven that causes him to crave more of what he has encountered. Saul (Greek name for Paul) is on the road to Damascus to hunt down Christians. On the way, Jesus shows up and gives him a taste of His presence. He then instructs Saul to go and wait for room service.

In the meantime, Saul goes to a house on Straight Street to prepare for breakthrough. Notice that he does not eat or drink anything for three days. He is fasting because he is only hungry and thirsty for the Kingdom. His hunger prepares him for the main course of breakthrough that Ananias finally brings after Saul waits for three days (see Acts 9:1-19).

We will be filled with what we are hungry for. If it is turkey, then we will get turkey. If we are consumed with hunger for a specific aspect of the Kingdom of God, then we will be filled with whatever we crave, whether it is healing, the prophetic, serving, wisdom, counsel, comfort, evangelism, teaching, giving, or something else. How much we are able to consume will depend on the size of our container.

For example, many Christians do not believe that they have the ability to heal the sick, and therefore, they have no hunger for that significant part of the Kingdom. Thus, they do not feast on that aspect of Kingdom resource. On the other hand, I have found that, when people do become hungry for God's Kingdom to come through healing, they eventually get breakthrough.

In Luke 11:9-13, Jesus says:

Ask and it will be given to you; seek and you will find; knock and the door will be opened to you.... Which of you fathers, if your son asks for a fish, will give him a snake instead? Or if he asks for an egg, will give him a scorpion? ...How much more will your Father in heaven give the Holy Spirit to those who ask Him!

HUNGER IN DISGUISE

Sometimes even critical questions can disguise our hunger. I'll never forget a time when an elder of the church that I had been ministering in approached me. The night before, we had seen many astounding miracles—blind eyes were opened, ears were restored, cripples were cured, tumors dissolved, and four cases of lupus were healed. It was an amazing night in which the goodness and kindness of God were unleashed on the church. Heaven was unlocked, and there was great rejoicing as a result.

One elder, however, did not like what was happening. He said, "I don't believe any of this! Nobody got healed last night! The people got scammed, and they're all going to have their symptoms return, getting worse, and they will eventually die!"

I was tempted to launch into a stellar defense of the authenticity of the miracles and healings of the previous evening. Instead, I responded, "So, when were you disappointed?"

He stared at me in shock. "How did you know?" he quizzed.

I went on to explain that often a critical, unbelieving spirit is born out of a feeling of hurt resulting from disappointment. In this case, it seemed obvious that he had sought God for a miraculous breakthrough of some kind and had not received what he had expected.

He conceded my observation, reciting a litany of friends who had not been healed or who had died after they had received prayer for healing, and then he boldly stated that he would not believe unless someone who he knew very well, and who he believed was credible, was healed.

I could sense that his skepticism was a result of disappointment and that he really wanted a reason to have hope restored, so I blurted out, "May you have a surprise supernatural encounter that will convince you of God's desire and ability to heal."

After dinner, a good friend, who he had reluctantly and nonchalantly prayed for the night before, approached him. She had left the meeting early because she was in so much pain, and she was not getting any breakthrough. Out in the parking lot, she approached this disgruntled elder, who was also leaving the meeting early in disgust, and asked him to please pray for her because she could not take the pain anymore.

She went on to say that, on the way home, all of the pain left her body, and for the first time in years, she was able to sleep through the night. She thanked him over and over, saying that he was the answer to her prayers for breakthrough!

Later in the meeting, I called out a word of knowledge for someone who had a bruise that God wanted to heal. It turned out that the youth pastor had had an accident two days before. He had fallen and broken a few ribs and was bruised from his chest to his hip. The skeptical elder had taken him to the hospital and knew firsthand the extent of his injuries.

The youth pastor's ribs were immediately healed, and the bruise completely disappeared. When the elder confirmed the miracle, he turned into a puddle of tears and began to testify to the greatness of God to the entire church!

The next day, he insisted on taking me to the airport. For an hour, he went on and on about how his hope had been restored, saying that God does respond to our hunger, even if it is masked in disappointment and a critical attitude. Finally, he declared that he was now committed to living a naturally supernatural life and to partnering with God for breakthrough in releasing the Kingdom of God!

Sometimes our questions are an indication of our hunger. "God, why isn't this working?" causes us to search out the answer. This gives God an opportunity to break through, like He did for the elder, and like He has done for me so many times when I have doubted. Fortunately, in the same way that He responded to Thomas (see John 20:24-29), Jesus does not get angry at us when we doubt—He just shows up.

God is looking for any opportunity to show up in our lives and circumstances. It is our hunger, however demonstrated, or even masked, that attracts His presence and power. Our hunger creates an atmosphere that unlocks Heaven, and the supernatural becomes a natural reality. Our hunger prepares the way for breakthrough. Who wants more?

ENDNOTE

1. James Strong, "Greek Dictionary," *The New Strong's Expanded Exhaustive Concordance of the Bible* (Nashville, TN: Thomas Nelson, 2001), "seek" (#1567).

Chapter 10

PARTNERING FOR BREAKTHROUGH

I entered into my first business venture at ten years old. It was a mobile car wash that my friend and I started in our neighborhood. We began our business with very little capital investment and minimal ongoing overhead—a hose, bucket, soap, sponge, and a couple of chamois—making for higher profit margins. It seemed like a sweet partnership—we were going to be *ten-year-old rich* together in no time!

I soon realized, to my chagrin, however, that our ideas of partnership were completely different. My idea of partnership was that we would do equal work for an equal share in the profit revenues. His idea was that I would do all of the marketing to get the business (knocking on doors), that I would wash the cars (while he held the hose to rinse, pointing out the places I had missed), and that I would dry (while he rinsed out the bucket and rolled up the hose). After three cars, I decided that I needed to form a new corporation. It had one owner and operator, and best of all, I kept all of the profits!

I learned early in life that a partnership requires both parties contributing commensurate to the ratio of revenue sharing. This is an earthly picture of the invitation that we have been given to share in heavenly rewards. The

Bible clearly teaches that each one of us will be rewarded for what we do here on earth. But if we desire to share in the spoils produced by the Kingdom (as it is released in people's lives), we must be prepared to do more than simply hold the hose (be carriers of God's presence) and point out where God has missed it (complaining that God did not come through)!

God has called us into a partnership with Him, which requires significant involvement on our part. Certainly, I am not suggesting that we are to work for our salvation. Rather, we must partner to release the Kingdom of God to earth. In other words, we must do our part in unlocking Heaven if we expect God to do His part in providing the power to release His Kingdom.

I used to have a 100-percent success rate in healing—I never prayed for anyone, and no one ever got healed! For many years, I truly believed that I was not gifted enough and did not have enough faith to see people healed through my prayers. When people came to me for healing, I would direct them to someone who was "gifted." Consequently, no one was ever healed through me.

My understanding of the "gift of healing" was that God sovereignly gave the gifts according to how He saw fit—if you had it, then you had it. If you didn't, then you didn't. It never occurred to me that I could access the gifts through hunger, as discussed in the previous chapter.

Jesus' command to heal the sick (see Matt. 10:8)—to release the Kingdom—was given to every believer, not just to the gifted. He gave this command to all 12 disciples when He sent them on their ministry trip, and He gave it again to all of the 72 when He sent them out (see Luke 10:9). In His final commission to His disciples, Jesus said, "These signs will accompany those who believe...they will place their hands on sick people, and they will get well" (Mark 16:17-18). Therefore, *every* believer is called to operate in the gift of healing.

God has called each one of us to partner with Him in releasing the Kingdom to those around us in whatever sphere of influence we find ourselves. Not only are we to partner in healing, but also in releasing *all* of the resources of the Kingdom, whether it is the prophetic, forgiveness, wisdom, revelation, comfort, service, or another aspect of Kingdom life. God's invitation into partnership with Him is not just a hopeful request. It is the responsibility of every believer. As Christians, it is up to us to unlock Heaven in order to provide Kingdom breakthrough for those who need God's intervention.

Go to the Interview

In Matthew 6:10, Jesus taught us to pray, "Your kingdom come, Your will be done on earth as it is in heaven." Unfortunately, many incorrectly quote this verse, adding *may* or *let* to the beginning: "[May] Your kingdom come, [let] Your will be done...." This, however, turns it into a hopeful prayer, rather than a declaration, as He intended it. Nothing in the Greek text warrants this sense of pleading for His Kingdom to come or hoping that He will somehow grant our request.

The problem with praying from this perspective is that it wrongfully relinquishes all of our responsibility for the outcome of breakthrough, placing it all on God and His supposed predetermined will. No wonder God gets the bad rap when things do not work out in people's lives the way they had hoped. We are relying on God to do what He is relying on us to do!

Further, the mood of the verb *come* is declarative. In other words, Jesus taught us to *declare* His Kingdom—"Your Kingdom come right now." As we discussed in Chapter 2, this declaration springs from the authority that we carry as royal sons and daughters. Jesus was teaching His disciples that they carried a responsibility to release the Kingdom. As authorized representatives, they must determine where and when it needed to come.

Additionally, Greek verbs have not just moods, but also tenses (when an action takes place), and senses (how the action happens—how it is completed). In Matthew 6:10, when Jesus taught His disciples to pray "come," He used the aorist verb tense/sense, which normally connotes a past tense and punctiliar sense (meaning a one-time occurrence). However, when the aorist tense/sense is used in combination with the declarative mood, as is the case in this verse, the verb tense changes from past to present, while the sense remains punctiliar, meaning a one-time occurrence.

In other words, Jesus was teaching that *we* would have to release the Kingdom every time that we needed to unlock Heaven and bring it to earth. Unlocking Heaven is not just a one-time prayer event that releases continual breakthrough for the rest of our lives or a futuristic prayer regarding the return of Christ. It is an ongoing, daily lifestyle of declaring His Kingdom coming wherever and whenever it is needed.

Sadly, some people approach Kingdom breakthrough like the man who continually asked God for a job. Every day, he complained that God was not keeping His promise to provide for his every need. Finally, after listening to a barrage of criticism regarding His supposed lack of concern, God said to the man, "Hey, I would like to provide you with a job, but it sure would help if you went to an interview!"

Sometimes we enter into a mistaken mindset that it is God's full responsibility to bring breakthrough in our circumstances. The release of the Kingdom in signs and wonders, miracles, healing, the prophetic, and supernatural evangelism, however, is contingent upon our decision to "go to the interview." We must be willing to partner with God for breakthrough.

Recently, after a Sunday evening service at Bethel Church, a 60-year-old woman approached me for healing prayer. This woman experienced chronic pain throughout her entire body and never seemed to get breakthrough, despite the fact that she had received prayer from everyone on our team several times.

I was exhausted from a full day's ministry, and I just wanted to go home, so I tactfully directed her to one of our Bethel School of Supernatural Ministry students, explaining that they could heal her just as easily as I could. The woman, however, pleaded with me to pray for her one last time before going home. Irritated, I reached out my hand toward her forehead and shouted out, "Well then, be healed. I release a 20-year-old body to you in Jesus' name."

At that, she threw her head back, let out an ecstatic yell, and promptly fell straight back onto the floor with a crack. I was concerned that she may have injured herself, but when she finally stood back up, she expressed that all of the pain had left her body—she was healed!

She explained that someone else had prophesied those very words just a few minutes before I had declared them over her. She went on to say that, when she heard the words for the second time, the presence of God came flooding into her, filling her entire body with healing ecstasy, and she could not stand under it. She was in utter shock as she stood, completely healed.

Even though I was irritated, reluctant, and had no sense of faith for this woman's condition, my decision to speak the words released the Kingdom in her body. She received a breakthrough because I chose to partner with God to release His presence.

Declaring "Your Kingdom come" is a responsibility that we have been given as members of the royal priesthood (see 1 Pet. 2:9). As priests of God, we are to declare His rule—His influence—wherever we see injustice; we are to mediate Heaven to earth and into every situation that needs God's intervention.

DECLARATIONS DETERMINE DESTINY

It is important for us to realize that, when we do declare His Kingdom coming, we are releasing Heaven to earth with our words. In fact, the Bible tells us that we have the power of life and death in our tongues (see Prov. 18:21; James 3:3-12). The reason Jesus warned us that we would be judged according to the words we speak (see Matt. 12:36-37) is that our words make a difference in people's lives and circumstances—our words can either curse or release the Kingdom to bring blessing.

Recently, I was backpacking in the Tahoe Desolation Wilderness area with some of the other pastors of Bethel Church. As we arrived at the trailhead, we were told by a group of guys who had just finished a week in the wilderness that we would not catch any fish. Everyone they met had shared the same sad tale.

Without hesitation, I declared, "But we have favor!"

Everyone laughed.

Amazingly, when we arrived at the first lake, the first cast produced a miraculous 14-inch rainbow trout! In fact, we caught so many fish every day that anything under 12 inches was thrown back. They were so plump that we were able to filet them into trout steaks. Each delectable bite resulted in rowdy rejoicing as we were reminded of the extreme favor that we had experienced from God through a simple off-the-cuff declaration.

It is important to keep in mind that our words, like those of Jesus, have authority. Often Jesus simply spoke to a situation or circumstance and Heaven invaded and brought change. In Matthew 8:26, He spoke to the storm, and the wind and the waves stopped. The disciples responded, "What kind of man is this? Even the winds and the waves obey Him" (Matt. 8:27).

The Roman centurion understood the authority that Jesus carried when he said, "...Just say the word and my servant will be healed" (Matt. 8:8). In response, Jesus declared, "Go! It will be done just as you believed it would" (Matt. 8:13).

Jesus spoke to the paralytic, saying, "Pick up your mat and walk," and the man did so and was healed (see John 5:8-9). Jesus stood outside Lazarus' tomb and spoke, "Lazarus, come out," and Lazarus was raised from the dead (see John 11:43). Our words (our declarations) create an avenue through which Heaven's resources and power are released.

I'll never forget an occasion when a woman, who was completely bald and gaunt from many radiation and chemotherapy treatments, approached me at a conference at Bethel. She explained that the doctors had told her that they could do nothing else for her and that she had approximately one month left to live. I immediately looked her in the eyes and declared, "I don't even need to pray for you. The glory of God is all over you; you're going to be just fine!" I went on to explain that my declaration over her was in response to a gift of faith that had come on me as I heard about the destiny of doom that the doctors had declared over her.

Five months later, at another Bethel conference, a shorthaired woman approached, grinning from ear to ear. She jubilantly shared that she was the woman whom I had declared life over. Thanking me profusely, she shared that not only was she obviously still alive, but that she also had no cancer in her body, to the amazement of the doctors!

As royal priests, representing God on earth, our declarations make a difference. Our declarations determine our destiny and the destiny of those around us. Our declarations unlock Heaven.

A Birdie

I was playing golf in Yuma, Arizona, with a pastor and his medical doctor friend who was very skeptical of the reality of divine healing. The pastor had arranged for us to golf together so that I could share testimonies that would convince the doctor otherwise.

By the sixth hole, we had not made much headway in convincing the doctor, even though I had shared several testimonies of people being healed in God's presence. The pastor teed off on the par three hole and hit a great-looking shot that was headed right toward the flagstick. Amazingly, and sadly, his ball struck a bird about 20 feet in front of the pin, causing both the ball and the bird to fall onto the green!

At first we were joking around about the pastor getting a literal birdie, but after realizing that the bird was lying on its side with its wing fixed straight up without moving, we became concerned that the bird was dead.

Meanwhile, the doctor and I hit up onto the green, while the bird continued to lie motionless. As we drove our carts toward the green, other birds landed near the dormant bird. Once we got to the green, all of the birds flew away, except for that one bird, still lying on its side.

Observing this, the doctor pronounced the bird dead. The pastor then expressed that he should dispose of it since, being a doctor, he seemed the most qualified to deal with the carcass. At that, I responded, "No way. Let's raise it from the dead." I then declared, "I release you into new life." Just when I got to "re," the bird jumped up and flew away!

The doctor looked at me in total shock as he witnessed the supernatural power of God firsthand. The bird was seemingly raised from the dead! Regardless of whether the bird was dead or just knocked out, the reality is that, as I declared God's Kingdom come, the bird recovered, and the doctor had no more problems with the issue of supernatural healing.

God is just waiting for us to co-labor with Him in releasing His Kingdom. Living naturally supernatural lives means simply unlocking the doors that lead to breakthrough with the Kingdom keys that we have received. Partnering for breakthrough, then, means that we take responsibility to release God's presence, power, and resources into every situation and circumstance in which people need His intervention.

That is the power of partnership. When we pray (declare), He comes.

WE HAVE THE KEYS

We have been given the keys to the Kingdom to be able to unlock Heaven whenever we need His presence and power. In Matthew 16:19, Jesus promised, "I will give you the keys of the kingdom...." In other words, we can unlock the door to the resources of Heaven to get whatever we need whenever we need it. That is an amazing privilege!

I oversee several ministry responsibilities at Bethel Church, which means that I have several different keys to access needed rooms and resources. There are several people on my leadership team who need to have the same access as I do. There was a time, however, when I was the only one with the keys.

Each time one of my team needed to access a room, he or she had to come to me and borrow the keys and then, afterward, would have to bring them back. Sometimes, he or she would forget, and I would have to go out of my way to track my keys down when I needed to access something. It got to be such a hassle trying to juggle one set of keys between our entire team that I finally wised up and got them their own keys!

Jesus did not say, "I will lend you the keys." Jesus *gave* us the keys, meaning that He no longer has them. It is now up to us to open up Heaven so that

His presence and power can be released through the opening that we have made for Him to come.

How often do we hear Christians pleading with God to open up the Heavens and rain down His power to intervene? All the while, God is pleading with us to use the keys that we have been given to release His rule so that intervention can come. We cannot expect God to do our job in the partnership.

When we do what is expected of us to unlock Heaven, then He faithfully does His part. It is His good pleasure to give us the Kingdom (see Luke 12:32).

Often, as I begin a conference, I announce that there will be many miracles and healings. The reason I am so confident is that I have been given Kingdom keys to unlock Heaven in order to access the resources needed. When I pray, He comes, and when He comes, He does good things because He is a good God in a good mood!

The natural question is, if we have the authority and power to represent and bring God's Kingdom to earth, why don't we see more breakthroughs in the miraculous?

Many Christians wrongfully believe that God just sovereignly intervenes in our lives whenever He chooses. When they don't experience breakthrough, their response is, "Well, I guess it was just God's will that I remain sick, debilitated, or dying." As a result, many Christians do not pursue divine intervention, or they stop short of getting the breakthrough they desire.

Many Christians believe that God chooses (predetermines) who will be healed and who will not be healed. They state that God is sovereign—that He is in control of everything—and, therefore, that nothing happens outside of His predestined will.

Therefore, if someone becomes sick, it must be God's will because nothing happens outside of His sovereign control. As a result, the prayer, "Your will be done..." is a concession to accept whatever God has sovereignly predestined, instead of a declaration: "...on earth as it is in heaven."

Purposes Are Predestined—Not People

Interestingly, the words *predestination* and *predestined* are only mentioned four times in the New Testament. In each of these instances, the predestination relates to the purposes of God rather than to people and their choices.

In Romans 8:29, for example, the apostle Paul writes, "For those God foreknew He also predestined to be conformed to the likeness of His Son...." This says that God has a predestined plan—being conformed to look like Jesus—for every believer. It is not saying that we are predestined to be Christians.

As Christians, God's will for us is that we become like Jesus in every aspect. There is no plan B for a Christian. God has already decided and committed Himself to conforming you into the image and likeness of Christ.

In Ephesians 1:3-12, Paul writes:

Praise be to the God and Father of our Lord Jesus Christ, who has blessed us in the heavenly realms with every spiritual blessing in Christ. For He chose us in Him before the creation of the world to be holy and blameless in His sight. In love He predestined us to be adopted as His sons through Jesus Christ, in accordance with His pleasure and will—to the praise of His glorious grace, which He has freely given us in the One He loves. In Him we have redemption through His blood, the forgiveness of sins, in accordance with the riches of God's grace that He lavished on us with all wisdom and understanding. And He made known to us the mystery of His will according to His good pleasure, which He purposed in Christ.... In Him we were also chosen, having been predestined according to the plan of Him who works out everything in conformity with the purpose of His will, in order that we, who were the first to hope in Christ, might be for the praise of His glory.

Notice that, in verse 4, we are chosen to be holy and blameless in His sight. In verse 5, we are predestined to be adopted as His sons (or daughters). Finally, in verse 12, we are predestined so that we might be for the praise of His glory. All three of these statements are pointed toward the purposes that God has for those who have chosen Christ. They are not about *who* God has predestined to follow Him.

Certainly, God knows us (foreknowledge) before we accept Him because He is not limited to time. He is outside of time and sees the past, present, and future in the eternal *now*. He is already seeing the choices that we have yet to make in the context of time, but that does not mean that He is dictating those choices in any way.

When Jesus said, "Many are invited, but few are chosen" (Matt. 22:14), He was not referring to those who are predestined, but to those who are in Christ, clothed in His righteousness. Jesus was pointing out that the only way that we will be able to stay at the wedding banquet in Heaven is if we have the right clothes on—the righteous robes of Christ. In other words, our good works and self-righteousness will not be appropriate covering to keep us in His presence. Only the blood of Christ can wash us clean and then cover us appropriately.

I believe the apostle Paul was referring to this concept when he penned Ephesians 1:4: "He chose us in Him...." In other words, there is no other plan for salvation other than the shed blood of Christ on the cross.

In the same vein of thought, the apostle Paul writes in Second Thessalonians 2:13, "...From the beginning, God chose you to be saved through the sanctifying work of the Spirit and through belief in the truth." In other words, the *means* of obtaining salvation was predetermined, not the people who would be sanctified and believe.

True, the plan for our salvation was determined before man was even created, but the way that we access this salvation is through our free will—our choice.

In the Garden of Eden, Adam was given free will—the ability to choose. Unfortunately, Adam chose unwisely, which allowed sin and death to enter the world through the open door created by that choice. Jesus, on the other hand, chose wisely in the Garden of Gethsemane when He submitted His will to the Father saying, "...Not as I will, but as You will" (Matt. 26:39). This choice opened the door for abundant eternal life to all who choose to live in Christ.

Hundreds of scriptural references emphatically detail the fact that God has given us the ability to freely choose our eternal destiny. For example, in Matthew 22:9, Jesus commanded, "Go to the street corners and invite to the banquet *anyone* you find." In Acts 2:21, we are promised that, *"Everyone* who calls on the name of the Lord will be saved."

WE CAN CHANGE GOD'S MIND

When Abraham came to Sodom and Gomorrah in Genesis 18, he contended to change God's mind about destroying those cities. His conversation with God went something like this: "If I can find 50 righteous men, will You change Your mind?" The Lord responded, "Yes, I'll change My mind and not destroy the cities."

Abraham continued to barter, "What if I can find 45?"

"OK."

"40?"

"Yes."

On a roll, Abraham continued going for more, until God finally agreed to spare the city if Abraham could come up with a mere ten righteous people. Unfortunately, he could not find them, but still, Abraham changed God's mind six times!

In Exodus 33, Moses changed God's mind about coming with him and the Israelites. In verse 17, the Lord said to Moses, "I will do the very thing you have asked, because I am pleased with you and I know you by name." Obviously God knows the names of His children (us), which grants us access to His presence, where we can change His mind about the things that affect our lives. Obviously, this is the goal of petitioning prayer: to influence God to change His mind.

In John 2:1-11, Jesus attends a wedding. During the party, the hosts run out of wine. Mary, knowing who Jesus really is, asks Jesus to provide wine. Jesus responds, "My time has not yet come." Without hesitation, Mary turns to the servants with the empty water jars and commands, "Do whatever He tells you." Her actions prompt Jesus to change His mind and move up the timing of His public ministry.

As a royal priesthood, I believe we are to intercede for the spiritual, emotional, relational, and physical needs of those around us. We are to be mediators between Heaven and earth, praying and performing God's will wherever it is needed.

When Miriam opposed Moses in Numbers 12, she contracted leprosy. Even though she brought the disease on herself through her rebellious actions, Moses sought God's power to reverse this curse after Aaron pleaded with him to intervene on her behalf. In verse 13, Moses petitioned, "O God, please heal her!" In other words, "Would You do this miracle for me?" The rest of the story implies that she was indeed healed after a seven-day cleansing period.

I constantly meet people who have made wrong decisions and are now paying the consequences with their bad health and debilitation. Amazingly, over and over, I have seen God's power come to heal them as I have mediated Heaven to earth on their behalf.

I'll never forget a guy I prayed for who had been smoking for 45 years and, as a result, had contracted emphysema. He could barely breathe, but after I mediated God's mercy over him for a few minutes, he began breathing normally, and all of the pain left. He began jumping up and down and then running and shouting that he had new lungs! Later, he testified that he felt like he had 20-year-old lungs!

Take Care of the Dog; Take Out the Trash

In the Garden of Eden, God commanded Adam and Eve to rule (see Gen. 1:26). They were responsible to rule in God's stead, even though God could have done it Himself. God gave Adam and Eve the privilege of partnering with Him so that they could experience the reward of influencing their environment.

It is just like in my house, where my daughter, Alexa, is the ruler of our dog, Chester. He's our dog, but she feeds him, gives him water, exercises him, and cleans up after him. Sure, I am certainly capable of doing each of those tasks, and I do them occasionally, but delegating the responsibility to her has helped her to grow in maturity and leadership, which is now translating into higher levels of opportunities to influence. At 16, she has already taught at conferences, led outreaches, and become a leader in her youth group.

God's predetermined will is that we "take care of the dog." Sure, on occasion, He does it Himself, but most of the time, as a good Father, He is patiently waiting for us to come into the fullness of maturity that we were created for. He is preparing us for greater levels of partnership with Him.

When I was a young teenager, one of my responsibilities around the house was to take out the trash. I did not have the same sense of priority as my parents, however, and had to be continually reminded to take the container to the trash cans outside. My normal response was, "I'll do it in a little while." Hours would go by until my parents would remind me again, and I would give the same reply. This was usually followed by threats of restriction, prompting me to reluctantly take care of my responsibility to take out the trash.

After a few months of this re-run every three or four days, my parents decided to stop enabling me. They just let the trash build up in the kitchen. Over three weeks or so, I had not even noticed the trash, until one morning I came downstairs and was greeted by 100 or so flies that had hatched in the garbage!

If there is one thing that I hate more than taking out the garbage, it is flies! I immediately went to my parents and asked them why they had let the garbage build up so much that it had created a *fly zone*.

They responded, "We were wondering when you were going to notice. We have decided that you have the capacity to determine when the trash needs to be taken out, and we will trust in your judgment."

I never let the trash get out of control again.

Many Christians wonder why God has allowed the "lord of the flies" to reign in our environment when all along He has given *us* the responsibility and the capacity to take the trash out! If we do not like what we are seeing, it is up to us to make a difference because God has given us the job and the capacity to do it.

In Matthew 10:8, Jesus commands, "Heal the sick, raise the dead, cleanse those with leprosy, and cast out demons." He did not say, "I'll heal the sick...." On the contrary, He tells His disciples to do it. The command implies the competency to perform the task. He is waiting for us to take out the proverbial trash!

The apostle Paul emphatically states in Second Corinthians 5:20, "We are Christ's ambassadors, as though God were making His appeal through us...." In other words, God has given us the responsibility to speak on His behalf, even though He is perfectly capable of doing it Himself.

God has given each believer the responsibility and authority to oversee everything that happens on the earth. In Matthew 10:1, Jesus gave the disciples authority to cast out demons and to heal every kind of disease, and in Matthew 28:18-19, He gave them all of His authority to carry out their responsibilities to release His Kingdom rule on earth.

Jesus is looking for people, today, who will choose to partner with Him in bringing Heaven to earth so that His will can be done on earth as it is in Heaven—so that the sick will be healed, the tormented will be set free, and salvation will come to everyone. Jesus is looking for laborers who will go to work in the harvest field because it is ripe for harvest (see John 4:35).

God's part in the partnership is providing the power for the miraculous. Our part in the partnership is choosing to stop for those who are hurting and then choosing to take risks in order to help them. God has sovereignly chosen to partner with us in bringing Heaven to earth. The question remains: will we fulfill our part in the partnership? Will we partner for breakthrough?

RECOMMENDED READING

The Ultimate Treasure Hunt
by Kevin Dedmon

A Life of Miracles
by Bill Johnson

Basic Training for the Prophetic Ministry
by Kris Vallotton

Basic Training for the Supernatural Ways of Royalty
by Kris Vallotton

Developing a Supernatural Lifestyle
by Kris Vallotton

Secrets to Imitating God
by Bill Johnson

Face to Face With God
by Bill Johnson

Here Comes Heaven
by Bill Johnson and Mike Seth

Loving Our Kids On Purpose
by Danny Silk

Purity—The New Moral Revolution
by Kris Vallotton

Release the Power of Jesus
by Bill Johnson

Strengthen Yourself in the Lord
by Bill Johnson

The Happy Intercessor
by Beni Johnson

The Supernatural Power of a Transformed Mind
by Bill Johnson

The Supernatural Ways of Royalty
by Kris Vallotton and Bill Johnson

When Heaven Invades Earth
by Bill Johnson

Additional copies of this book and other
book titles from DESTINY IMAGE are
available at your local bookstore.

Call toll-free: 1-800-722-6774.

Send a request for a catalog to:

Destiny Image₀ Publishers, Inc.
P.O. Box 310
Shippensburg, PA 17257-0310

*"Speaking to the Purposes of God for This
Generation and for the Generations to Come."*

**For a complete list of our titles,
visit us at www.destinyimage.com.**